As one of the world's longest established and best-known travel brands, Thomas Cook are the experts in travel.

For more than 135 years our guidebooks have unlocked the secrets of destinations around the world, sharing with travellers a wealth of experience and a passion for travel.

Rely on Thomas Cook as your travelling companion on your next trip and benefit from our unique heritage.

S0-AHW-930

WITHDRAWN

Thomas Cook **pocket** guides

TURKEY
MEDITERRANEAN COAST

WEST PALM BEACH PUBLIC LIBRARY
411 CLEMATIS STREET
WEST PALM BEACH, FL 33401
(561) 868-7700

Thomas Cook

Your travelling companion since 1873

Written by Lindsay Bennett; updated by Robin Gauldie

Published by Thomas Cook Publishing
A division of Thomas Cook Tour Operations Limited.
Company Registration no. 3772199 England
The Thomas Cook Business Park, Unit 9, Coningsby Road,
Peterborough PE3 8SB, United Kingdom
Email: books@thomascook.com, Tel: + 44 (0)1733 416477
www.thomascookpublishing.com

Produced by Cambridge Publishing Management Limited
Burr Elm Court, Main Street, Caldecote CB23 7NU

ISBN: 978-1-84848-264-7

© 2006, 2008 Thomas Cook Publishing
This third edition © 2010
Text © Thomas Cook Publishing
Maps © Thomas Cook Publishing/PCGraphics (UK) Limited

Series Editor: Adam Royal
Production/DTP: Steven Collins

Printed and bound in Spain by GraphyCems

Cover photography © World Pictures/Alamy

All rights reserved. No part of this publication may be reproduced, stored in
a retrieval system or transmitted, in any form or by any means, electronic,
mechanical, recording or otherwise, in any part of the world, without prior
permission of the publisher. Requests for permission should be made to the
publisher at the above address.

Although every care has been taken in compiling this publication, and the contents
are believed to be correct at the time of printing, Thomas Cook Tour Operations
Limited cannot accept any responsibility for errors or omissions, however caused,
or for changes in details given in the guidebook, or for the consequences of any
reliance on the information provided. Descriptions and assessments are based on
the author's views and experiences when writing and do not necessarily represent
those of Thomas Cook Tour Operations Limited.

CONTENTS

WHAT'S IN YOUR GUIDEBOOK?

Independent authors Impartial, up-to-date information from our travel experts who meticulously source local knowledge.

Experience Thomas Cook's 165 years in the travel industry and guidebook publishing enriches every word with expertise you can trust.

Travel know-how Thomas Cook has thousands of staff working around the globe, all living and breathing travel.

Editors Travel-publishing professionals, pulling everything together to craft a perfect blend of words, pictures, maps and design.

You, the traveller We deliver a practical, no-nonsense approach to information, geared to how you really use it.

● *View of Cleopatra Beach, Alanya*

INTRODUCTION
Getting to know Turkey's Mediterranean coast

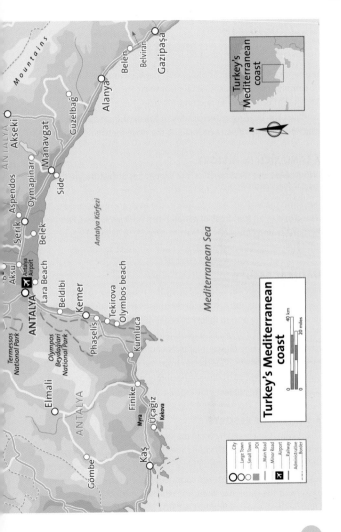

Turkey's Mediterranean coast

Mediterranean Sea

Antalya Körfezi

Mountains

ANTALYA

Akseki
Aspendos
Serik
Oymapinar
Manavgat
Güzelbağ
Side
Belek
Aksu
Antalya Airport
ANTALYA
Lara Beach
Beldibi
Kemer
Tekirova
Olympos beach
Kumluca
Phaselis
Termessos National Park
Olympos Beydağlari National Park
Elmali
Finike
Üçağiz
Myra
Kekova
Kaş
Gömbe
Belen
Belviran
Gazipaşa
Alanya

Turkey's Mediterranean coast

N

City
Large Town
Small Town
POI
Main Road
Minor Road
Airport
Railway
Administrative Border

0   40 km
0   20 miles

Getting to know Turkey's Mediterranean coast

Is your idea of the perfect holiday destination long, hot sunny days? Beautiful sandy beaches? Crystal-clear seas? Friendly people? Lots to see and do, but no rush to do anything? 'Buzzing' nightlife or a quiet evening with just the buzzing of the cicadas? A touch of spice but with a few touches of home? If so, then Turkey is the place for you.

A LAND RICH IN HISTORY

'Where East and West meet' or 'the Crossroads of History' are just two ways to describe this land. Turkey stretches from the Aegean Sea in the west into the Middle East and Asia in the east, and it has been used as a land bridge for hundreds of generations. Persians, Greeks, Romans, Byzantines and Ottomans all feature strongly in its long history and have left fascinating legacies for today's holidaymakers to explore.

NATURAL BEAUTY

Not a history buff? No worries! Turkey has much more to offer. The Mediterranean region has one of the most varied landscapes in Turkey. In the west, the 3,000 m (9,843 ft) peaks of the Taurus and Olymbos mountains form a dramatic backdrop for the resorts, but as you travel east the mountains retreat inland, leaving a wide and dusty coastal plain. The mountains offer shelter from the harsh Siberian winds that cut across inland Turkey during the winter, giving Antalya and its close surroundings the mildest year-round climate in the country.

A VARIETY OF RESORTS

The region is anchored by three major 'mega' resorts, each with a different character. Antalya, the capital of the region, is a city with a life outside tourism and a cosmopolitan atmosphere, while Side is a pure resort town with a very mixed continental clientele. Alanya, the most easterly of the three, has two great beaches and a magnificent citadel. Outside these you will find Turkey's first purpose-built resorts – Belek

🔺 *The Taurus Mountains are the highest in Turkey*

and Kemer being the most popular – set in the finest locations and with a great range of up-to-date sports facilities. From all these resorts a wealth of excursions awaits.

EVENING ENTERTAINMENT

How to fill the balmy evenings? The large towns offer some of the most raucous nightlife of any holiday destination in Europe – great foam parties and fishbowl cocktails – while smaller resorts are the perfect locations for romantic meals and moonlit strolls on the beaches. Or you could always head to a Turkish bath for a little pampering.

THE BEST OF TURKEY'S MEDITERRANEAN COAST

The Turkish Mediterranean offers a wealth of fantastic experiences that fill the hours from just after dawn until well after dusk.

TOP 10 ATTRACTIONS

- **Explore Kaleiçi in Antalya** Take a daytime stroll leading to drinks overlooking the harbour as the sun sets in the medieval heart of this sophisticated resort (see page 29).

- **Views from the citadel at Alanya** Get a bird's-eye view of the coast from the battlements of this impressive 13th-century fortress (see page 17).

- **Explore atmospheric Side** Where past meets present (see page 35).

- **Tee off at Belek** You will not feel under par after a round on these excellent courses (see page 50).

- **The theatre at Aspendos** An awe-inspiring example of Roman architecture still being used today (see page 62).

- **White-water rafting in Köprülü Canyon** Sheer exhilaration (see page 65).

- **Barter for a bargain at the bazaar** Shopping is theatre in Turkey, designed to both entertain and lighten your wallet (see page 30).

- **The flames of Chimaera** View one of mother nature's hottest spectacles (see page 77).

- **The lost city of Termessos** The 'hidden' city that thwarted Alexander the Great (see page 66).

- **Go hot-air ballooning** over the rock spires of Cappadocia or the ruins of Aspendos (see page 89).

🔽 *Inner courtyard of Kızılkul (Red Tower) fortress by Alanya's harbour*

SYMBOLS KEY

The following symbols are used throughout this book:

ⓐ address ☎ telephone ✆ fax ⓦ website address

🕐 opening times ❶ important

The following symbols are used on the maps:

𝒊 information office		○	city
✉ post office		○	large town
⬛ shopping		○	small town
✈ airport		◼	POI (point of interest)
✚ hospital		—	main road
🛡 police station		—	minor road
🚌 bus station		—	railway
╱ city walls		---	administrative border
❶ numbers denote featured cafés, restaurants & evening venues			

RESTAURANT CATEGORIES

The symbol after the name of each restaurant listed in this guide indicates the price of a typical three-course meal without drinks for one person:

£ = under 25 YTL   ££ = 25 YTL–100 YTL   £££ = over 100 YTL

▶ *Alanya castle and views*

RESORTS
Places under the sun

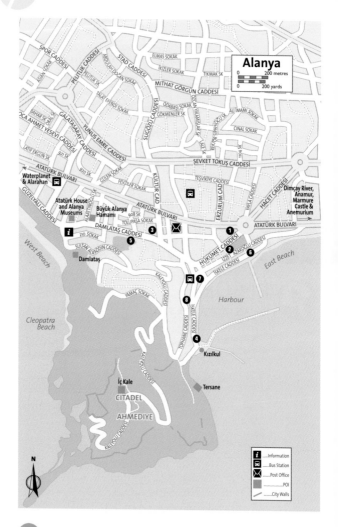

Alanya

0 ——— 200 metres
0 ——— 200 yards

SPOR CADDESI
STAD CADDESI
ELMAS SOKAK
TİKİZLER SOKAK
TİKMAK SK
PELİTLİK CADDESİ
ABDULLAH DOĞAN SOKAK
PELİTLİK SK
MITHAT GÖRGÜN CADDESİ
TALAT EFENDİ SOKAK
OĞABAŞI SOKAK
DOĞAN TARAKÇILAR SK
ALİ İMAM SOKAK
BAHAR SK
GALATASARAY CADDESİ
YUNUS EMRE CADDESİ
SUÇÖZÜ CADDESİ
GÖKMENLER SK
BEYZ SİPAHİOĞLU SK
LATİF SK
CİNAL SOKAK
HOCA AHMET YESEVİ CADDESİ
ŞIT SK
LATİF ERGÜN SK
GÜLEN SOKAK
ŞEVKET TOKUŞ CADDESİ
DİÇA SK
GÜZELYALI CADDESİ
ATATÜRK BULVARI
TEŞVİKİYE CADDESİ
Waterplanet & Alarahan
FEVZİLER SOKAK
KÜLTÜR CAD
ATATÜRK BULVARI
ERZURUM CADDESİ
KRTA CADDESİ
HACET CADDESİ
Dimçay River, Anamur, Marmure Castle & Anemurium
Atatürk House and Alanya Museums
Büyük Alanya Hamamı
KALETHOCA SK
908 SK
TOLLUPAŞA SOKAK
DAMLATAŞ CADDESİ
3
ATATÜRK BULVARI
i
210 SOKAK
5
HÜKÜMET CADDESİ
1
İZZET AZAKOĞLU CADDESİ
2
6
SULTAN ALAADDIN CADDESİ
Damlataş
West Beach
İSKELE CADDESİ
East Beach
KALEİÇİ CADDESİ
YAMAÇ SOKAK
7
8
Harbour
Cleopatra Beach
TOPHANE CADDESİ
İSKELE CADDESİ
4
Kızılkul
İç Kale
KALEYOLU CADDESİ
Tersane
CITADEL
AHMEDIYE
KALEYOLU SOKAK
N

i ....Information
.............Bus Station
✉ ....Post Office
■ ....POI
╱ ....City Walls

Alanya

One of Turkey's most easterly tourist resorts, Alanya has a high rocky promontory that is one of the most dramatic along the coast. The 250 m (820 ft) high precipice has a magnificent citadel that was the focus of the town for centuries.

Flanking the promontory like long golden wings are two exceptional beaches that are the main draw as far as holidaymakers are concerned. A ribbon of hotels, bars and restaurants now fans out on either side of the town, so whichever accommodation you choose you are never far from refreshment and entertainment.

Aside from the tourist strip along the coast, restaurants and nightlife are clustered in a triangle between the harbour front, **İskele Caddesi** and **Hükümet Caddesi** in the shadow of the citadel. You can take a quiet meal across from the fishing boats before diving into the sometimes raucous bars and clubs that stay open until the early hours.

The main thoroughfare, **Damlataş Caddesi**, links old Alanya with the new town. Lined with trees and street cafés and boutiques, it has an atmosphere similar to that of a French boulevard. The side streets, with their small shops and market stalls, offer a total contrast – here you can bargain for that must-have souvenir among the hustle and bustle.

HISTORY

Founded as a Greek colony, Alanya became a renowned pirate base in the 2nd century BC because it was easy from here to target the ships carrying valuable cargo across the eastern Mediterranean from Cyprus and Egypt. The Romans were not happy about this and eventually sent a naval force to crush the rebels in 67 BC.

In 44 BC Roman general and would-be emperor Mark Antony gave the town to his lover and political ally, Cleopatra, queen of Egypt. Unfortunately for them, they were beaten by rivals within the empire and, according to legend, Cleopatra took her own life by allowing herself to be bitten by an asp (a venomous snake). The town was a southern bastion of the Christian Byzantine Empire, but was taken by the Muslim

Seljuks in 1221; their first sultan put the final touches to the magnificent castle, making it his naval base and winter home.

Alanya tourist office ⓐ Damlataş Cd 1 ⓣ 0242 513 1240

BEACHES

Alanya's town beaches are impressive. Sitting either side of the citadel, they have been given the rather unromantic names East and West Beach.

West Beach is the longest, at 8 km (5 miles), and this is where the vast majority of the new tourist development has taken place, a thin ribbon of hotels, restaurants and bars stretching into the distance. The beach has all the usual tourist amenities, including a full range of watersports.

East Beach is only 3 km (2 miles) long but is still longer than the beaches at many other resorts in Turkey. It tends to be a little quieter than West Beach and attracts more local people, especially at weekends.

Cleopatra Beach sits in the shadow of the citadel and is the smallest of the town beaches. It does not have the level of amenities of the other two, with simple snack bars and cafés, but there are volleyball courts here, and competitions are held during the summer.

THINGS TO SEE & DO

Alanya Museum

Although the museum has the usual range of ancient remains, plus photographs of where they were found, the best part of the museum is the collection of Ottoman relics. There is a re-creation of a traditional Ottoman living room and some old farming implements in the garden.
ⓐ Hilmi Bağcı Cd at Damlataş Cd ⓛ 08.00–12.00 & 13.00–17.30 Tues–Sun; closed Mon ⓘ Admission charge

Atatürk House and Museum

Atatürk, founder of the Turkish republic and national hero, made a fleeting visit to Alanya in the 1920s and stayed in this house, which is now

preserved as a museum. Today, the downstairs rooms pay homage to Atatürk with photographs and documents. The upstairs part of the house may be more interesting to foreign tourists. It is furnished in the typical style of the early Turkish republic, which flourished in the 1920s and 1930s.
ⓐ Hilmi Bağcı Cd at Damlataş Cd ☎ 0242 513 1228 🕐 08.30–12.00 & 13.30–17.30

Büyük Alanya Hamamı

A Turkish bath with sauna, jacuzzi, hairdresser and bar – so not exactly traditional. ⓐ Damlataş Cd at Alaattinoğlu Sk ☎ 0242 511 3344
❗ Admission charge

Citadel

The setting of the citadel in Alanya is one of the most dramatic in Turkey. Built high on the sheer rocky peak that separates the two beaches, it was considered impregnable in medieval times.

Ahmediye This old village within the citadel nestles around the walls of İç Kale (see below). There is a 16th-century mosque and some atmospheric old Ottoman houses, but they are difficult to explore because of the sea of cotton and linen festooned along the alleyways. The women here used to crochet and make lace by hand and sell it to tourists. Today, most of it is machine made and even imported, although you can still buy some lovely table sets as souvenirs. There are numerous small cafés where you can enjoy a drink before you head back down into town.

İç Kale At the very top of the citadel's peak is the Inner Castle, or İç Kale, built in 1226. This was the military and political headquarters of Seljuk leader Alâeddin Keykubad. The walls remain almost intact, and from here the panoramic views down the hill, over the town and beaches and both east and west along the Mediterranean coast, are truly breathtaking. Stand on a small platform in the northwest corner. This is where prisoners were once thrown to their deaths.

SHOPPING

Alanya town There is a wide range of goods to be found within Alanya's main shopping area (off Damlataş Caddesi towards the harbour and around the main bus station), but also a fair amount of T-shirts, jeans and designer rip-offs. More upmarket boutiques – particularly those selling locally produced silk, which is a speciality of the town – can be found on Damlataş Caddesi itself.

Ahmediye village In the citadel, this is the place to shop for lace and table linens, which bedeck every alleyway and shop front.

Market Held weekly, on Fridays, this is a huge affair and fills the streets around the *dolmuş* (bus) station.

🕐 09.00–21.00 (summer); 09.00–18.00 Tues–Sun (winter)
🛈 Admission charge

Outer Citadel A total of 7 km (4½ miles) of walls are draped around the slopes of the hill. These are held together by around 150 towers set at strategic lookout and entry points. The garrison lived within these lower slopes, and it included hundreds of foot soldiers and their families, blacksmiths, cooks and laundry workers. You can see the ruins of their military village on the approach road to the inner castle.

Damlataş

You can reach Damlataş, or the Cave of the Dripping Stones, from land, and it is one of the most impressive caves in the area, with spectacular stalactites and stalagmites. The constant temperature and damp air of the caves is said to be good for people with asthma.

ⓐ Off Damlataş Cd 🕐 10.00–sunset 🛈 Admission charge

Harbour

The lovely inner harbour at the foot of Kızılkul (see opposite) is home to scores of small, colourful fishing and pleasure boats. You can watch the fishermen mending their nets or just relax at one of several cafés.

Kızılkul (Red Tower)

Kızılkul was built as part of the harbour defences in 1226, the same year as İç Kale. The name comes from the red stone of its octagonal walls. There is a small ethnological or lifestyle museum inside, but more exciting are the views across the harbour from the top battlements.

ⓐ On the harbour front ⓣ 0242 512 3255 ⓛ 09.00–18.00 Tues–Sun; closed Mon ❶ Admission charge

Tersane

The shipyard, or *tersane*, was erected by the Seljuks to build and repair their shipping fleet. This is said to be the only shipyard of its age still found in Turkey.

ⓐ On the harbour to the south of Red Tower ⓛ 24 hours

Waterplanet

This water park has 23 slides and rides, a 350 m (383 yd) artificial river for rafting, wave pools, bars, restaurants and a discotheque.

ⓐ Okurcalar Mevkii, Manavgat (30 km/19 miles from Alanya on the way to Side) ⓣ 0242 527 5165 ⓦ www.waterplanet.com.tr ⓛ 08.00–18.00 (closing times vary with season) ❶ Admission charge

EXCURSIONS
Alarahan

Hans were wayside inns built during Seljuk times for the camel and horse trains that carried goods across Asia. Alarahan was built in the 13th century at the foot of a pass through the Taurus Mountains on the banks of the River Alara by Seljuk Sultan Alâeddin Keykubad. It did not alter much until it underwent a massive renovation in the late 1990s.

It is a job well done because the architects have not messed about with the basic structure. You can still see the stables where the animals were tethered and the communal sleeping and eating chambers for the men. The building is open as a museum and café during the day, with a great sitting area on the roof. In the evenings it hosts Turkish evenings with traditional foods and dancing.

● *The citadel at Alanya is situated high on a sheer rocky peak*

The ruins of a Byzantine fortress sit on a rocky outcrop above the *han*. There is a footpath up there, but it is not well used and the climb is steep in parts. Allow four hours if you want to attempt the trip.
ⓐ 39 km (24 miles) west of Alanya, inland from the main 400 coast road
ⓒ 10.00–01.00 ❶ Admission charge

Anamur

It is a full-day trip to reach Anamur on the coast, but worth it for history lovers.
ⓐ 110 km (68½ miles) east of Alanya

Anemurium

Located on a spit of land that is the southernmost tip of Turkey are the remains of Anemurium, an important late-Roman and Byzantine city, abandoned in the 7th century when Arab forces took control of Cyprus and began sacking settlements along this coast. The site has not been fully excavated, but offers some excellent mosaics and monumental public buildings.

ⓐ East of Alanya, just west of Anamur town ⓛ 08.00–20.00 (summer); 09.00–17.00 (winter) ❶ Admission charge

Boat trips to the caverns & Cleopatra Beach

The rocky outcrop of the citadel is cut with caverns, particularly on the southern edge bounded by the sea. Many of the small boats in the harbour offer two-, three- or five-hour trips to see the caves. These are at their best in the late afternoons when the sun lights up the insides.

The tour often includes **Phosphorus Cave**, where the water glows an eerie green; **Lover's Cave**, where it is said a German woman and her Turkish boyfriend hid from the police for three months in 1965; **Pirate's Cave**; and **Cleopatra Beach**, directly under the citadel, where the Egyptian queen came to bathe during her romance with Mark Antony.

ⓐ Alanya Harbour ⓛ 09.00–sunset ❶ Admission charge

The Dimçay River

The Dimçay River runs out of the Taurus Mountains to the sea and it is the place to come for freshwater swimming or to enjoy a lunch or dinner of fresh trout, kebaps or *gözleme* (see page 100) at the cafés that line the banks. The tables are set on wooden platforms in the cool river shallows. Don't be surprised to find the water pretty chilly!

ⓐ 6 km (4 miles) from the city centre ⓛ 24 hours

Marmure Castle

The remains of Marmure Castle are some of the best on the Turkish coast. Built by the Byzantines and expanded by Alâeddin Keykubad, who built the citadel at Alanya, it has a romantic setting on the water.

The crenellated walls saw action up until the beginning of the 20th century and are so authentic that they are often used as a film set for Turkish films.

ⓐ East of Anamur Ⓛ 09.00–17.00 ⓘ Admission charge

TAKING A BREAK

Gaziantep Park £–££ ❶ A civilised spot, near the Atatürk statue, to enjoy a light lunch or just an ice cream or maybe a Turkish liqueur.
ⓐ Hükümet Cd Ⓣ 0242 512 8843 Ⓛ 09.00–23.30

Mahperi ££ ❷ A restaurant that has been in business for decades, so you know it is of a good standard. The waterfront setting is lovely. The menu concentrates on fish, but you can also order the less expensive range of kebaps. ⓐ Gazipaşa Cd Ⓣ 0242 512 5491 Ⓛ 11.00–23.00

Eski Ev £££ ❸ Meaning 'Old House', this is one of the finest restaurants on this part of the coast. The dining room of the converted mansion is the perfect place to enjoy grand Turkish cuisine, or you can take a table out in the garden. ⓐ Damlataş Cd 44 Ⓣ 0242 511 6054
Ⓛ 18.00–23.00

İskele £££ ❹ Set in the tiny harbour, İskele is slightly more expensive than its neighbours but the service is a little more refined and worth it if you want to dress up and make an event of it. The menu concentrates on fish and seafood. ⓐ İskele Cd at Tersane Sk Ⓣ 0242 511 0304
Ⓛ 11.00–24.00

Ottoman House £££ ❺ One of the best addresses in Alanya, this restaurant has had a loyal following for years. Set, as the name suggests, in an old Ottoman mansion, it serves good Turkish cuisine, including slow-cooked lamb and *meze*. You can dine in the garden or on one of the terraces. ⓐ Damlataş Cd 31 Ⓣ 0242 511 1421 Ⓛ 17.00–23.00

AFTER DARK

Bistro Bellman ⑥ Bistro Bellman is Alanya's largest open-air disco and its trendiest venue. Close to the harbour, it is set on two tiers and has five bars, several dance floors, and cool terraces with sofas. The DJ concentrates on the latest chart dance tracks and pop. It is also open for dinner (until midnight) and serves Turkish, European and Latin dishes, and has great views over the harbour. ⓐ İskele Cd 4 ⓣ 0242 512 1992 ⓛ 12.00–03.30

James Dean ⑦ Ten bars set on four different dance floors, with plenty of opportunity to either dance or relax in comfortable sofas and seating areas. Around the side you will find the entrance to The Doors: a lounge bar with an old Chevy hanging from the ceiling. ⓐ İskele Cd Rıhtım Sk 32 ⓣ 0535 337 3242 ⓛ 20.00–04.00

Janus ££ ⑧ Bar and disco is downstairs while upstairs there is a fish and steak restaurant. ⓐ Rıhtım Cd ⓣ 0242 513 2694 ⓛ 11.00–23.00 (restaurant); 23.00–03.00 (disco)

⬥ *Alanya Harbour*

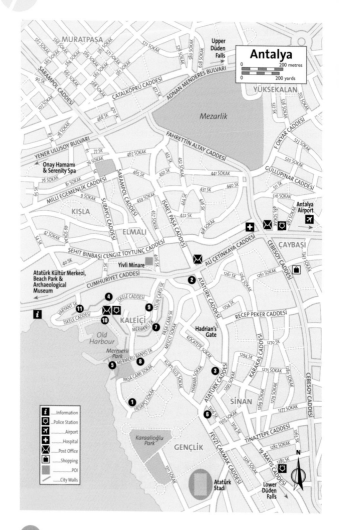

Antalya

The anchor city of the Mediterranean coast, Antalya is, aside from Istanbul, the most 'happening' city in Turkey, with a university and new, hi-tech industries attracting a young, energetic and high-earning population. It is the perfect place to capture the 'East meets West' spirit that is modern Turkey.

Set on a wide, sandy bay backed by the ruggedly beautiful Taurus Mountains, Antalya has a wonderful location that has been the focus of many a passing conqueror. It is also in the sunniest part of Turkey, where temperatures stay comfortable throughout the winter – perfect for an early or late trip.

Antalya's tourist attractions act as a magnet for holidaymakers from all along the coast. The old town, Kaleiçi (see page 29), is a large medieval enclave, its cobbled streets and Ottoman mansions dripping with atmosphere, while at its waterside, the Roman harbour is the focal point of boat trips by day, evening strolls and the city's famed nightlife. Further history beckons at the Archaeological Museum (see page 27), which is the best in southwest Turkey.

Despite its size, Antalya has a lively international tourist strip west of the downtown area away from the urban sprawl, taking advantage of the long beach. Here you will find all the watersports and holiday activities you would expect at the vast Beach Park (see page 26), but the 'buzzing' city is just on your doorstep.

Antalya tourist office ⓐ Cumhuriyet Cd 90 ⓣ 0242 241 1747
Tourist information line ⓣ 0800 511 07 07/08

HISTORY

The Persians founded Antalya in 158 BC on the site of a deep natural harbour. This was an important port throughout ancient times, and was prized by the Romans and Byzantines because it was safe and gave them easy access to the whole eastern Mediterranean. When the Ottomans took over the city in the 16th century, it was surrounded by a 5 km (3 mile) long wall. They divided it into four districts housing the Greek,

Jewish and Muslim communities, and also the ruling classes, or Mamelukes. After the fall of the Ottoman Empire, the harbour was still an important port, but Kaleiçi – the old town within the walls – lost its commercial role and its mansions became dilapidated.

BEACHES

Konyaaltı is a long, wide bay stretching out west of the city centre along the shoreline of the Gulf of Antalya. Konyaaltı now fronts Antalya's expanding 'hotel district'. The whole section is actually split into 12 differently named pebble beach areas, each with its own access, cafés and activities, which range from watersports to beach volleyball and soccer.

The attractions of the **Antalya Beach Park** (see opposite) are also just on hand. There is a shelf just offshore here, so make sure you keep young children and non-swimmers to the shallows. To the east of town, beach activities tend to centre on several private beach clubs (🛈 Admission charge) with no sand but artificial lidos. They are not ideal for younger children, but perfect for those who do not like getting sand mixed with their sun lotion. The closest one to the city is the **Adalar Club**, which you can reach from Karaalioğlu Park. **Mermerli** beach is another small stretch of sand and pebbles southeast of the harbour wall.

Lara Beach is sometimes referred to as if it is separate from Antalya, but really it is a suburb of Antalya (it is only 17 km/10½ miles to the east of the city centre), and many of the city dwellers head here at weekends to enjoy the fantastic beach and watersports.

There are many informal beach bars backing the strand, so you can simply spend the day on the beach, but Lara has other attractions, including what was Turkey's first water park (🌐 Dedeman Hotel, Lara Yolu 🛈 0212 275 7600 🌐 www.hotellarabeach.com). This has a range of rides, pools and activities for adults and children of all ages. The Dedeman Hotel also has a bowling alley, which is pretty unusual for Turkey, and might make a change for a family evening out.

THINGS TO SEE & DO

Antalya Beach Park

Antalya Beach Park to the west of the downtown core is a pre-planned leisure area with a wide range of children's activities that also suit adults. The major attraction is **Aqualand**, a water park with rides, a wave pool, an activity pool with caves to explore, plus an area of 650 sq m (780 sq yds) for children under six to play.

ⓐ Dumlupınar Bl, Konyaaltı Koruluğu Yanı ⓣ 0242 249 0900
ⓦ www.beachpark.com.tr

Antalya Archaeological Museum

This is one of the best archaeological museums of ancient finds in the eastern Mediterranean, with artefacts from sites all around the region. The main collections worth viewing – many of them are given their own rooms – are as follows:

⬤ *Hotel Lara Beach resort*

Finds from Perge The highlight of the museum is the collection of artefacts from the ancient city of Perge to the east of Antalya (see Excursions, page 58). The highly decorated monumental statuary (mostly 2nd century AD) shows how sophisticated the city must have been in its heyday. The collection of ornamental friezes that decorated the theatre at Perge is to be considered the finest of its kind in the world.

Bronze Age finds Items here date from the 8th to the 6th centuries BC, when the Phrygian people inhabited the area. Keep an eye out for the exquisite statuary and funerary urns. There are also finds from the ancient cave complex, the Karain Cave – the earliest populated site yet found in Turkey (see page 68).

Byzantine & Christian items The prize item here is the reliquary that is said to have held the bones of the 4th-century Bishop of Myra, St Nicholas, or Baba Noel, as he is known in Turkish, the saint on whom the modern legend of Santa Claus is based (see Excursions, page 73).

Ethnological Collection This room holds a fine collection of Seljuk and Ottoman handicrafts, with a diorama of a traditional nomadic lifestyle showing how many Turks lived until the 20th century (and, in fact, how some still do).
ⓐ Hilmi Bağcı Cd, Damlataş ⓣ 0242 513 1228 ⓛ 08.00–17.30 Tues–Sun; closed Mon ⓘ Admission charge

Atatürk Kültür Merkezi/AKM (Antalya Culture Centre)
This huge exhibition complex – a copy of the Louvre pyramid in Paris – is the basis of Antalya's cultural life, hosting the International Film Festival and regular plays and concerts, with everything from pop to the Antalya Symphony Orchestra. With its lovely parkland, this is the place to come for a stroll or to take tea at one of the cafés.
ⓐ 100 Yıl Bl ⓣ 0242 244 0328 ⓛ 10.00–18.00 & in the evenings for performances

City walls

Various sections of the old city walls survive. At the main entrance to Kaleiçi, Kalekapısı, a section of wall, supports Saat Kulesi, a Seljuk clock-tower. Other sections run from the harbour around the rocky coastline, but the longest and most impressive stretch runs south of Hadrian's Gate.

Hadrian's Gate

This is one of the best-preserved monuments in Antalya. Built on the eastern flank of Roman Antalya in AD 130, this triumphal arch celebrated a visit to the city by Emperor Hadrian. A flight of steps leading down to the gate shows just how much higher the modern city is than the one that existed in Roman times.

Kaleiçi

This labyrinth of narrow alleyways and courtyarded mansions is still evocative of Ottoman Turkey, although today the quarter is home to stylish boutique hotels, upmarket restaurants and bohemian shops. There is no set route; just follow your nose around the next picture-perfect corner, browsing as you go. You will be able to explore excellent renovations or evocative ruins, but whether the mansion is a palace or the pits, the beauty is in the detail – wooden lintels, stone archways and a palate of weather-worn pastel stucco walls add to the atmosphere.

Mermerli & Karaalioğlu parks

A welcome place to relax under the shade, the parks offer tea rooms and play areas for children. Think of them as somewhere to cool off after your tour of the old town.

Old harbour

Down on the shore below the mansions of Kaleiçi, the harbour is now a pleasure marina with a flotilla of little boats offering tours of the bay. There are several cafés and restaurants, so it is a popular place for an early evening drink or dinner. While you are relaxing you can examine the walls of the harbour, which were built by the Romans, although they

SHOPPING

Antalya is famous throughout Turkey for its jams and preserves. **Halk Pazarı**, or People's Market, does a great line in designer fakes, but is also the permanent fruit and vegetable market for the city. Or try **Pazar**, which has the usual range of Turkish souvenirs and also a refurbished traditional gold market, **İki Kapılar Hanı**. There are some great shopping venues in Kaleiçi, often renovated mansions housing bohemian boutiques and carpet shops. This is the place to buy an unusual item rather than mass-produced souvenirs. The atmosphere is a little less frenetic than in the tourist bazaars and prices are generally higher.

Antalya has some excellent modern shops that cater directly to its young affluent urbanites. A wander along Atatürk Caddesi and Işıklar Caddesi is as exciting as any high street back home and a little more glitzy than most.

The **Migros Shopping Centre** on Bulvarı Arapsuyu Mevkii is one of a new breed of American-style shopping malls with a huge hypermarket, 96 shops and an entertainment centre.

The 'duty-free zone' next to the modern port west of the city also has a modern mall-style shopping area.

have been reinforced regularly since then, and watch young and old out for a stroll in the cooler evening air.

Turkish baths & spas

For a relaxing break from sightseeing and sunbathing, try a Turkish bath or spa.

Onay Hamamı This is the most authentic Turkish bath in the city centre. ⓐ 47 Sk at 100 Yıl Bı ⓣ 0242 244 0908 ⓛ From 05.00 (men) & 08.00 (women); closes at 24.00

Serenity Spa This is a well-equipped spa with mud-chamber massages, exfoliations and body treatments. There is also a traditional

hamam, jacuzzi and sauna. ⓐ Sheraton Voyager Hotel, 100 Yıl Bı
ⓣ 0242 238 5555 Ⓦ www.starwoodhotels.com

Turkish Night

A Turkish dinner followed by the Mevlana Dervish dancers, folk dances
and a belly-dancing show. Pick up at 19.00 and a return to your hotel
at 23.00.

Mevlana Tours ⓣ 0242 243 6950 Ⓦ www.mevlanatours.com

Yivli Minare (Fluted Minaret)

Built in 1230 by Sultan Alâeddin Keykubad, Yivli Minare, so-called because
the minaret has a fluted tower, has become a symbol of Antalya. The
mosque next door is still used for worship.

EXCURSIONS

Boat trips

Head to the old harbour, where a flotilla of boats offers tours out into
the Gulf of Antalya or to the beach at Konyaaltı. A popular destination is
the lower Düden Falls (see below).

Düden Falls

A lovely area of several cascades surrounded by some verdant
landscapes, the Düden Falls make a perfect excursion from the city. The
lower Düden Falls are the most impressive, dropping 30 m (98 ft) directly
into the Mediterranean Sea. A crowd of tour boats visits every day from
all around the Gulf of Antalya to watch the spectacle.

To visit the upper falls 9 km (5½ miles) inland you can take a *dolmuş*
or rent a car. The multiple cascades are surrounded by verdant
woodland with lots of places to enjoy a picnic and tea gardens for
refreshment. You can walk directly behind the cascade, which is a
thrilling experience.

The falls are always busy on summer weekends when families from
Antalya visit for an afternoon of relaxation.

ⓐ 15 km (9½ miles) north of Antalya Ⓛ 08.00–sunset ❶ Admission charge

TAKING A BREAK

Castle Café & Bar £ ❶ Clifftop setting makes the journey a rewarding one; come here for the views, the ambience and the inexpensive food and drinks. ⓐ Hıdırlık Sk ❶ 0242 242 3188

Dönerciler Çarşısı (Döner Market) £ ❷ This popular area has lots of cheap *döner* and *pide* stalls and as a result has become known as the '*döner*' market'. It is a place for young Turks to hang out and meet their girlfriends and boyfriends. No stall really stands out, but it is a great place to stop for a quick, cheap lunch during your sightseeing trip. ⓐ Cumhuriyet at Atatürk Cd ❶ 08.00–01.00

Gül ££ ❸ A Turkish/German-owned restaurant frequented by locals and resident expats. Offers a good range of traditional dishes that are well cooked and not overpriced, and you can relax in the garden for a pleasant lunch or dinner. ⓐ Kocatepe Sk 1 ❶ 0242 247 5126 ❶ 11.00–24.00

Hisar Teşişleri ££ ❹ This restaurant is set in the ramparts of the old town, and has a terrace overlooking the bay. You therefore come here as much for the views as for the food – both of which are excellent. ⓐ Cumhuriyet Meydanı, Kaleiçi ❶ 0242 241 5281 ❶ 11.00–16.00 & 18.00–24.00

Mermerli Restaurant ££ ❺ This excellent seafood and grill restaurant's biggest asset is its own tiny pebble beach (complete with sunbeds and umbrellas) on the tiny bay just south of the Old Harbour. ⓐ Mermerli Banyo Sokak 25 ❶ 0242 316 5307 ⓦ www.mermerlirestaurant.com ❶ 11.00– 24.00 daily (Jun–Sept); 12.00–15.00 & 20.00–24.00 daily (Oct–May)

Stella's Bistro ££ ❻ Having been around for a few years now, this restaurant knows how to cook a steak and there are other non-Turkish meals on the menu. ⓐ Fevzi Çakmak Cd 3 ❶ 0242 243 3931 ❶ 11.00–22.00

Sirri Restaurant ££–£££ ❼ The beautiful Ottoman décor of this renovated mansion with its verdant garden sets the scene for your meal in this restaurant. The menu concentrates on fresh fish and typical dishes like delicious *güveç*. ⓐ Uzun Çarşı Sk 25, Kaleiçi ⓣ 0242 241 7239 ⓛ 11.00–24.00

Kırkmerdiven (40 Steps) £££ ❽ The menu concentrates on meat grills, either typically Turkish or European in style, with various sauces. Eat in the air-conditioned dining room or out on the shady terrace. Either way, the Ottoman music accompanying your meal will be a pleasant change from the latest Euro pop. ⓐ Mermerli Sk, Selçuk Mah ⓣ 0242 242 9686 ⓛ 11.00–24.00

AFTER DARK

Akdeniz Çiçek Pasajı ❾ Visit this restaurant-club for a taste of authentic traditional Turkish music (and occasional belly dancing which is considerably more authentic than the version you will encounter at your hotel's 'Turkish night'. ⓐ Uzun Çarşı Sk 24/26, Kaleici ⓣ 0242 243 4303

Club Arma ❿ This is Antalya's most sophisticated nightspot and the dance area is unique because of its proximity to the sea. ⓐ Kaleiçi Yat Limani, Iskele Kaddesi 75, Old Harbour ⓣ 0242 244 9710 ⓦ www.clubarma.com.tr ⓛ 19.30–03.00

Disco Alli (Ally) ⓫ Open-air disco that is the place to be in the city, with foam parties, laser shows and eight bars. It sprawls across land around the Roman walls in the old part of town. ⓐ Musalla Sk, Selçuk Mah, Kaleiçi ⓣ 0242 244 7704 ⓛ 22.00–04.00

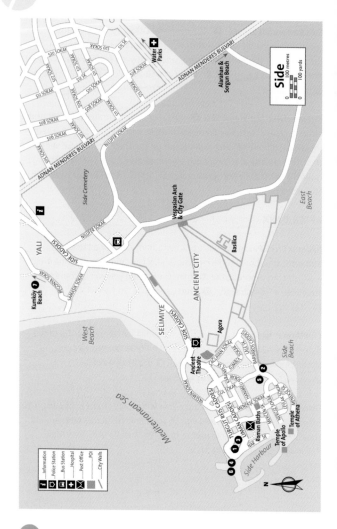

Side

Side (pronounced See-day) means 'pomegranate' in an ancient Anatolian dialect – although no one is really sure why this was used as a place name. Today, Side is unique along the Turkish coast; an ancient site wrapped in a modern, bustling holiday resort.

The compact town centre sits on a rocky promontory that is closed to traffic in the evenings. It is an atmospheric mix of shops, restaurants and bars that is perfect for a simple stroll or some serious bar crawling. Either side of the promontory, the long, sandy beaches are great for bronzing and watersports. The western side of town is most developed, with a ribbon of hotels backing the strand. From here it is a stroll along the beachside promenade into the heart of Side.

Side combines everything that is good about a holiday in Turkey – some great ancient history that is not too overwhelming, good beaches and cheeky banter from the shopkeepers, who sell the whole range of Turkish souvenirs, plus great nightlife from chic bars to noisy nightclubs. ❶ If you have a rental car, do not park it on the approach to the town, because it will be towed away. Use the large and inexpensive car park just before the pedestrian area.

HISTORY

Side was one of the major slave markets in the area from soon after it was founded in the 7th century BC. Sacked by Arab forces in the 7th century AD, it was still occupied in the 11th century but was then abandoned, perhaps after earthquake damage. The site was not resettled until the 1920s, by Muslim fishermen from Crete who came after the exchange of populations between Greeks and Turks. It remained a quiet fishing port until the arrival of tourism.

BEACHES

The rocky promontory where you find the town centre is flanked by good beaches. West of the town there is a long, slender beach reaching for several kilometres around the bay, and this is where the hotels and apartments were built in the 1970s and 1980s. The eastern beaches are wider and until the 1990s were totally unspoilt. Several larger hotel complexes offering generally more upmarket accommodation have recently been built. There is also a small, rocky beach on the south side of the promontory off Barbaros Caddesi. For beaches further afield, take a *dolmuş* to **Sorgun** (3 km/2 miles east) and **Kumköy** (10 km/6 miles west).

THINGS TO SEE & DO

Agora

This was the site of the main slave market in the Greek era, but the most interesting building here is the remains of a Roman, 24-seat communal latrine – people were not as shy in those days as they are now!

Ancient road

Situated between the baths and the *agora* (and on the modern approach road into town after the tourist office), there are interesting sections of the ancient colonnaded road that was the main access to the town.

Ancient theatre

Whereas most of Turkey's ancient amphitheatres are built into hillsides, Side's is totally free-standing and makes a very impressive sight. Built by the Greeks, it was expanded by the Romans to seat 15,000. The interior has an interesting feature – a wall around the orchestra, built to protect audiences from the wild animals used in gladiatorial contests and to allow the orchestra to be flooded to hold mock naval battles.
ⓐ At the entrance to the modern town ⓛ 09.00–18.45
ⓘ Admission charge

Basilica

Relatively near the theatre (see above) and *agora* are the remains of a large early Christian basilica with some wonderful Romanesque architecture such as columns and small, arched windows. Part of the site has been taken over by bars and cafés, offering some of the most romantic and atmospheric settings in Side for a pre- or post-dinner drink.

City walls

Sections of the Roman city walls run down each side of the promontory and across the landward approaches. Some are free-standing, but others are now disguised by more modern architecture. It is always worth keeping a lookout for the walls as you stroll around the town.

Roman baths

The well-preserved Roman baths have been converted into the Side Museum and they now display a selection of fine statuary discovered at the site, and hundreds of pieces of decorative friezes and bits of stonework that really bring to life how attractive the city must have looked a couple of thousand years ago.

ⓐ Side Museum, in town centre ⓛ 08.00–12.00 & 13.00–17.00 (summer); same hours Tues–Sun (winter) ❶ Admission charge

🔺 The Temple of Apollo at sunset

Side Harbour

A tiny harbour, with stone outcrops (ancient artificial breakwaters) at either side that give the Side promontory the look of a crab with its claws out, is the home of some lovely wooden tour boats and the odd fishing vessel. It is the place for an evening stroll, and is lined with bars and restaurants ranging from basic eateries to relatively exclusive, upmarket places. Prices are more expensive than in the town streets, but you pay for the views.

Temples of Apollo & Athena

Set in a lovely position just by the water, these two 2nd-century AD temples make an atmospheric place to come and watch the sun set. Some of the stonework has been re-erected to form an arch decorated with extremely fine carved detail.

Vespasian Arch & City Gate

This marks the entrance into the town even in modern times. It has a fine, carved pediment on top of its Corinthian columns.

Water parks

Club Ali Bey Manavgat Aquapark Part of a holiday village complex, with a range of pools, rides and slides.
ⓐ Manavgat Alanya Karayolu, Manavgat ❶ 0242 748 7373
Ⓦ www.clubalibeymanavgat.com.tr ◐ 08.00–18.00 (closing times vary with season) ❶ Admission charge

Waterplanet With 23 slides and rides, a 350 m (383 yd) artificial river for rafting, wave pools, bars, restaurants and a disco, this is a well-thought-out water park with something for the whole family. ⓐ Okurcalar Mevkii, Manavgat ❶ 0242 527 5165 Ⓦ www.waterplanet.com.tr ◐ 08.00–18.00 (closing times vary with season) ❶ Admission charge

EXCURSIONS
Alarahan

It is worth the trip to see this town with its nearby ruins (see page 19).

SHOPPING

Barriers at the upper end of town limit traffic, and the main pedestrian streets of the downtown core offer some of the best and most typical tourist shopping in the region – it is to all intents and purposes a bazaar, but with shops rather than stalls. You will find everything here from gold to leather to carpets, plus the usual piles of T-shirts and socks. It is a very atmospheric place, especially in the evenings.

A line of simpler stalls selling pottery, cheap jewellery and other budget items stretches out around the bay on the West Beach boardwalk.

Boat trips

The most popular boat trip from Side is to the waterfalls at Manavgat (see below).

If you have your own transport, head upriver from the falls. You can lose the crowds and there are some lovely shady cafés or riverside picnic sites where you can spend time playing in the fresh water.

Manavgat Şelalesi (Manavgat Waterfalls)

Niagara Falls they are not, but these tumbling, picturesque cataracts surrounded by verdant gardens make a refreshing trip from the sometimes stifling coastal strip.

Several sets of horseshoe falls – the highest of these has a 3 m (10 ft) drop – cleanse the air with cooling water vapour, and there is a large café/tourist site nearby for refreshments and (mostly) tacky souvenirs.

The boat trip up the Manavgat River from Side (or the shorter trip from the town of Manavgat) is a lovely way to spend a day just watching the river banks pass by.

Weekends are often very busy as the falls are a popular picnic site for Turkish families from the surrounding area.

⬤ *Side Harbour*

TAKING A BREAK

The End ££ ❶ This restaurant's location justifies its name, but to be sure of a table at a terminal point facing the sea you'd best make a reservation. ⓐ Liman Cd ⓣ 0242 753 2005 ⓦ www.theendside.com ⓛ 10.00–12.30

Moonlight ££ ❷ As the name suggests, this is an open-air restaurant, where you eat by candlelight on the water's edge – perfect for a romantic meal for two. The menu has fish and a range of European dishes, including some vegetarian options. ⓐ Barbaros Cd 49 ⓣ 0242 753 1400 ⓛ 11.00–01.00

Ottoman Restaurant ££ ❸ The best value on the harbour – this restaurant still attracts local clientele, which is always a good sign. The Ottoman serves Turkish cuisine and seafood, so come and try something a little different. ⓐ Liman Cd ❶ 0242 753 1434 ⓛ 11.00–01.00

Aphrodite ££–£££ ❹ This restaurant on the main square has been here a while so it must be reliable, although it is a bit more expensive than its neighbours. The menu has the usual meats and fish, plus a special fish stew cooked in a clay pot that needs to be pre-ordered. ⓐ Liman Cd ❶ 0242 753 1171 ⓛ 08.00–24.00

AFTER DARK

Spanning late September and early October, a music festival hosts its evening shows in the ancient theatre. Contact the tourist office for details (❶ 0242 753 1265) or check the posters displayed outside the theatre.

The Blues Bar ❺ A bar with great live music and the usual lively bar atmosphere. ⓐ Cami Sk ❶ 0242 753 1197 ⓛ 19.00–03.00

Lighthouse ❻ This unusual setting for a bar fires out high-energy music right across the town every night. ⓐ Liman Cd, on the northern side of the promontory by the harbour ❶ 0242 753 3588 ⓛ 22.00–03.00

Oxyd ❼ The place to be on this part of the coast, it is a massive open-air space with a capacity of 3,000 and several different-style areas, including a swimming pool. You can get transport out there but it is a taxi ride back. ⓐ Denizbükü Mevkii, 3 km (2 miles) west of the town centre on West Beach ❶ 0242 753 4940 ⓦ www.disco-oxyd.com ⓛ 22.00–04.00

Kemer, Beldibi & Tekirova

Kemer is one of the earliest government-approved, and therefore carefully planned, tourist developments to have sprung up along the Turkish coast since the late 1980s. This narrow corridor of the land southwest of Antalya had never had a large natural population, but was ripe for tourist development. A great beach, pristine waters and a magnificent backdrop of pine-clad rocky peaks were the idyllic natural stage on which to build a resort.

The resort itself, however, is not one of the most picturesque places – lots of functional, white-painted concrete – but what Kemer lacks in charm it makes up for in facilities, including an upmarket marina that attracts a wealthy international clientele.

Everything for a fun beach holiday is here, plus classy shopping – although the nightlife is a little more laid-back than further east along the coast. Over time, development has expanded along the coast with other small resorts at Beldibi and Tekirova. These have a predominance of large, all-inclusive resort hotels, and Kemer is the lively heart of the 'strip'.

○ *Kemer Moonlight Park Beach*

HISTORY

Kemer was the site of the ancient city of Idyros, or Likya, but nothing of this remains and little is known about it. By the early 20th century there was only a simple village on the site, but it suffered flooding from rain from the Olymbos Mountains. To counteract this, the local people built over 20 km (12½ miles) of walls to protect the village. Kemer means 'belt' in Turkish – the name comes from these protective structures.

BEACHES

Kemer's long but narrow pebble beach is jam-packed with loungers and umbrellas all summer. The only sandy beaches are found at **Moonlight Park**, in front of **Yörük Parkı** and next to the **marina**. Wooden jetties in front of each of the main hotels offer watersports and extra sunbathing space.

THINGS TO SEE & DO

Diving
Aksuna Sports There is some good diving just offshore, and this company has a good reputation and operates from the marina. It also has other activities.
ⓐ Kemer ⓣ 0242 814 5132

Horse riding
Hotel Berke Ranch This equestrian centre is also a hotel and offers one- and two-week packages with daily rides, but you can also book lessons or head out on a trail for an hour or two. There are 26 horses and the complex covers 18 ha (45 acres) of forest.
ⓐ Akçasaz Mevkii, Kemer ⓣ 0242 446 0333
ⓦ www.hotel-berkeranch.com

Kemer Marina
This is one of the finest modern marinas along the Turkish coast, with berths for 300 yachts and other boats. There are some fantastic and

extremely expensive craft here and it's the perfect place to enjoy the maritime atmosphere and watch the activities of the crews and clients.

Moonlight Park Beach

Most of what Kemer has to offer in terms of what to do happens here. The long, sandy beach is a major draw, but add to this some good activities and a collection of restaurants, cafés and shops, and you have somewhere you can spend the whole day. The following sections are certainly worth a visit:

Amphitheatre A 500-capacity, traditionally styled open-air venue that hosts cultural shows during the day and converts into a cinema in the evenings – this generally shows international films, but with Turkish subtitles.

Mini-Club A programme specially designed for youngsters where they get to play games and enjoy arts and crafts, so parents can leave them knowing they are fully supervised.

Swimming pool A large, freshwater pool for those who do not want to swim in the sea.

Naturland

This offbeat theme park (and hotel accommodation) is unique in Turkey, and also offers thalassotherapy treatments and a traditional Chinese wellness centre with massage, acupuncture and medicinal treatments. Its main highlights are:

Aquarium Park This is a combined aquarium and water park where you can watch the sea life of the Mediterranean in its salt-water home (the first of its kind in Turkey), and then enjoy an hour or so having fun on the water slides and in the freshwater pools, take diving lessons or simply enjoy the beach with its watersports.

Country Park An ecological and folkloric reserve where the organic farming practices of old rural Turkey have been rekindled. At the cafés on site you can eat food made with the crops grown here. There are also colourful parades, magic shows and circus acts.

Forest Park Here you can learn all about the forest ecosystem. It is a fun approach, with parks for youngsters and interactive activities for older children and adults. There is also a life-size re-creation of Noah's Ark with models of the animals.

ⓐ Çamyuva, Kemer ⓣ 0242 824 6214 ⓦ www.naturland.com.tr
ⓛ From 08.00 (closing times vary with season) ❶ Admission charge

Turkiz Hotel Thalasso Centre

This hotel's large thalassotherapy spa offers a luxurious variety of treatments, including endermology, pressotherapy and seaweed therapy, plus numerous sea-water programmes. There is also a *hamam*, steam room, sauna and fitness centre.

ⓐ Yalı Cd 3, Kemer ⓣ 0242 814 4100 ⓦ www.turkiz.com.tr

Yörük Parkı (Nomad Park)

This themed parkland area re-creates the traditional lifestyle of the nomadic Anatolian Turks, and you can enjoy fresh *gözleme* made by the ladies while the traditionally dressed men serve *ayran* yoghurt drinks to wash it down. It is a wonderfully cool and relaxing place to visit after a day of bronzing on the beach.

EXCURSIONS
Boat trips
Several boat trips from the main marina head out to **Olymbos beach** (see page 76) and to **Phaselis** (see below).

Phaselis
Founded by Greek colonists from Rhodes in the 6th century BC, Phaselis was a major port and trading city for several hundred years. Today the ruins of the city lie among heady pine forest and are interspersed with pretty sandy coves, some of which used to be the old city harbours. You can do a little exploring in between sunbathing, snorkelling and swimming. Under the water you can explore the walls of the old port – now a home for fish and the odd small octopus.

● *Remains of the fine amphitheatre at Phaselis*

Boat trips along the coast drop you at the site, or there is road access with a ticket office and a small museum and refreshment kiosk – but taking a picnic is better. Note that Phaselis gets very busy at weekends, with families coming here from Antalya, so, for a quieter time, visit during the week.

ⓐ 15 km (9½ miles) south of Kemer ⓒ 08.00–19.00 (summer); 08.00–17.30 (winter) ❶ Admission charge

TAKING A BREAK

Monte Kemer £££ Favoured restaurant of the World Rally teams when they are in town, Monte Kemer does great steaks. ⓐ Atatürk Cd 41 ❶ 0242 814 6226 ⓒ 11.00–24.00

AFTER DARK

Nightlife in the region tends to revolve around the hotel discos and most of the large complexes have one – music tends to be in the bland, Euro-pop style.

Aura A large, open-air club with laser and light shows that is the heart of after-midnight action in Kemer. Regular theme nights and foam parties add to the fun. ⓐ Deniz Cd 3 ❶ 0506 409 4040 ⓒ 22.00–03.00 (summer)

Club Inferno Big open-air club next to Aura. ⓐ Deniz Cd 1 ❶ 0242 814 5332

Navigator Bar This bar is the focal point for the yachting crowd. With many expats living on board their boats throughout the year, it is busy throughout the seasons. Great atmosphere with wonderful views across the hundreds of masts. ⓐ Yat Limanı, in the marina ❶ 0242 814 1490 ⓒ 08.00–01.00

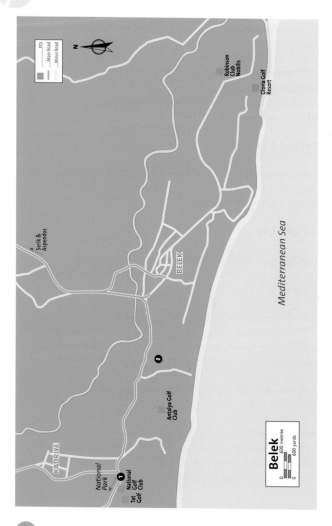

Belek

Mediterranean Sea

Robinson Club Nobilis

Gloria Golf Resort

Serik & Aspendos

BELEK

Antalya Golf Club

KADRIYE

National Park

National Golf Club

Tat Golf Club

N

POI
Main Road
Minor Road

0   600 metres
0   600 yards

Belek

With over 300 days of sunshine each year and temperatures that rarely drop below 10°C (50°F), this sheltered corner of the Mediterranean coast was chosen in the mid-1980s as the site of a new, purpose-planned resort. This was a new concept for Turkish tourism – huge 4- and 5-star hotel complexes offering full board or all-inclusive packages with a high level of service and a whole range of activities on site.

It has been a huge success, and Belek has quickly gained a reputation in the marketplace as a great all-year-active resort. The sporting facilities here attract the main Turkish football teams, Galatasaray and Fenerbahçe, for pre-season training, along with an increasing number of European teams including Spartak Moscow.

For information on Belek and links to the golf clubs see
ⓦ www.belektourismcenter.com

⬥ *The pristine fairways of a golf course at Belek*

BEACHES

Belek sits on the western stretch of a fine, sandy beach that runs all around the bay to Antalya (30 km/19 miles away). The beach is especially suitable for families and for swimming. Ranks of sunbeds and umbrellas stretch as far as the eye can see, and there are watersports operators in front of each of the big hotels on Belek's seafront.

THINGS TO SEE & DO

Golf

Antalya Golf Club Opened in 2003, Antalya Golf Club has state-of-the-art facilities and a particularly good golf school, with special provision for junior players. There are two courses here, the par-71, 6,411 m (7,013 yd) **Sultan**, and the par-72, 5,731 m (6,270 yd) **Pasha**, both designed by European Golf Design and consultant David Jones.
ⓐ Uçkum Tepesi Mevkii, Serik ❶ 0242 725 5970
ⓦ www.antalyagolfclub.com

Gloria Golf Resort Opened in 1997, this 18-hole, par-72, 6,296 m (6,888 yd) course was designed around several lakes and runs through pine forest and along the shoreline of the 5-star full-service Gloria Resort Hotel. A 9-hole course was added in 2001.
ⓐ Acisu Mevkii ❶ 0242 710 0600 ⓦ www.gloria.com.tr

National Golf Club This par-72, 6,232 m (6,818 yd) course was designed by professional golfer David Feherty and was the first to be opened here, in 1994. It has held several international tournaments. There is also a 9-hole, par-29 course, and 40 driving ranges.
ⓐ Serik ❶ 0242 724 4620

Robinson Club Nobilis The largest resort in Belek, the Nobilis has an excellent range of sporting facilities set around its upmarket villas and holiday club accommodation. It has a golf academy staffed by

PGA-qualified professionals. The course, designed by Dave Thomas, borders the Acısu River and makes the most of the natural terrain.
ⓐ Acisu Mevkii ☎ 0242 715 1491

Tat Golf – International Golf Club Tat features three separate 9-hole courses that can be combined to an 18- or 27-hole round. The Tat, Belek and International 9s each have a par of 36 with a length of around 3,200 m (3,500 yds).
ⓐ Uçkum Tepesi Mevkii ☎ 0242 725 5303

Spas
Gloria Verde Resort & Spa The thalassotherapy spa here specialises in 'thalgo' treatments using plant extracts imported from France in conjunction with sea-water therapies. It also has a full range of massage and wellness treatments (ⓦ www.gloria.com.tr).

The Robinson Club Nobilis Offers a full package of wellbeing programmes, be it diet, fitness, meditation or body therapies. It has licensed trainers as well as systematically designed programmes, and a bistro that will prepare meals tailored to your programme (ⓦ www.nobilis.com.tr).

Watersports
Belek caters to all kinds of watersports. Most of the major hotels run their own watersports rental and instruction centres. These are also open to non-residents.

EXCURSIONS
Birdwatching
Data collected to date has revealed that of approximately 450 bird species known in Turkey today, 109 are found in this region. Certain of these species are on the verge of extinction or highly endangered. Of particular recent interest was biologists' breeding of the endangered *Tyto alba* (hooded owl). **Ezop Travel** (based in Istanbul) offers birdwatching trips. ⓦ www.ezoptravel.com

Fire of Anatolia

This breathtaking dance show takes place at the newly built Gloria Aspendos Arena, next to ancient Aspendos. Ⓦ www.fireofanatolia.com
❶ Tickets from all major hotels in Belek and Antalya

Turtle spotting

The beaches around Belek are a favoured nesting spot for turtles (*Caretta caretta*), and most hotels offer guided walks.

Zeytintaşı Cave

Discovered by accident in 1997, Zeytintaşı is a massive two-level cave some 14 m (46 ft) below ground with exceptional columns, stalactites and stalagmites. It is famed for its 'macaroni' stalactites – long, thin strands of hardened calcium that hang from the cave roof.
ⓐ 28 km (17½ miles) inland, near Serik Ⓛ 09.00–18.00
❶ Admission charge

TAKING A BREAK

The Park Café £–££ ❶ Overlooking the lake and the 18th hole of the National Golf Club, the Park Café is a relaxing place for a late breakfast, lunch or afternoon snack. The menu offers international light meals and snacks, but also a delicious selection of traditional Turkish food, including *gözleme* cooked as you watch. ⓐ Belek Turizm Merkezi, Serik Ⓣ 0242 724 4620 Ⓦ www.nationalturkey.com Ⓛ 11.00–17.00

Roman Bar and Restaurant ££ ❷ This is the one place in the resort where you can sit down with a cold beer and watch Sky Sports, or enjoy an evening of karaoke with your friends. The place to come if you're looking for the English crowd. ⓐ Cumhuriyet Cd 8, Kadriye, Belek
Ⓣ 0242 725 5363 Ⓛ 10.00–03.00

❍ *Ancient rock-carved tombs in Anatolia*

EXCURSIONS
Out & about

Around the Mediterranean

There are various ways to get out and about beyond your resort, to give you a chance to see the traditional Turkish way of life and discover the countryside around.

THINGS TO SEE & DO

Gület cruise

It's really not a true Turkish holiday if you don't get out onto the water. From offshore you can really appreciate the beauty of the landscape, the verdant pine forests, olive groves and unspoilt beaches and coves. You may even be lucky enough to spot a dolphin or a turtle.

The traditional Turkish wooden boat – a *gület* – is one of the most beautiful and distinctive crafts in the Mediterranean and you will find them in all Turkish ports. You can rent them privately, but why bother – there's a vast choice of day trips available for very reasonable prices. You can enjoy lunch and take a swim before returning to your resort at about 17.00 or 18.00 in time to shower and change for your evening meal.

Jeep or 4x4 safari

The jeep safari is a real adventure, taking you out and about on roads you would probably never find by yourself in a rental car. The day includes a traditional lunch and a spot of shopping at a craft market or carpet warehouse. Two possible routes are:

Western Lycian peaks From Kemer and the west there are exciting routes into the western Lycian peaks behind the resort, with high mountain scenery along roads that traverse the mountain ridges. Routes from Antalya can follow the same roads, or head north into the Taurus Mountains where the coastal plain meets the Anatolian landmass. The Köprülü Canyon (see page 65) is a popular site.

Around Side & Alanya The coastal plain is much wider at Side, so the scenery is less dramatic than in the west of the region, but there are compensations because there are far more rural communities here, plus a couple of good carpet cooperatives where you can see traditional methods of silk and wool production, natural dyeing and weaving. Alanya may share some of the same routes as Side, or you may head into the hills to the *yaylas*, or summer resorts, where the Ottomans would come to spend time in the cooler air away from the oppressive heat of the coast.

Turkish baths

Not only will you be squeaky clean and relaxed, but your suntan will last far longer. What better reason to try a traditional Turkish bath, or, as the locals call it, a *hamam*?

History Cleanliness is very important in Islamic cultures, where face, hands and feet must be clean before each prayer session. The communal *hamams* were a place where hot water could be guaranteed and where men or women could come and have a good gossip. During Ottoman times it was grounds for divorce if a man refused his wife bath money. Today, although many town houses and apartments have all the mod cons, it is still a popular social activity.

What to expect Traditional *hamams* have separate sessions for men and women, but the owners of *hamams* in tourist areas understand that visitors have different attitudes and will run mixed sessions. When you enter a *hamam* you are given a *peştamal* (gown) and wooden sandals to wear. You can go naked under the robe or wear a swimming costume, bikini or shorts.

Then you go into the *hararet*, or steam room, where you are hit by a wall of hot air. Go to one of the basins and wash yourself all over. When you wash the suds off, do not get any back in the basin because this needs to be kept clean for other customers. You then lie on the *göbek taşı*, or navel stone, the marble slab at the centre of the room. Relax for 15 minutes or so to let the heat open up the pores.

Your masseur or *tellak* will then rub you with a rough cloth covered in soap to slough off any grime and dead skin cells. Then you are

pummelled and rubbed until you feel as though your arms and legs might fall off. After another shower, you leave the hot room, wrap yourself in a thick robe and relax with a cup of tea. Do not rush this part because you need to cool down and let your body adjust to the treatment.

A Turkish evening

Genuine Turkish food and entertainment may be difficult to find in many modern resorts, but the 'Turkish evening' offers the perfect introduction to the culture. You will start with a buffet meal of *meze* dishes, barbecued meats and salads washed down with local wine or beer, after which you will be entertained by folk dances, plus of course the famous 'belly dance'. Someone from the audience is always invited to have a go, which is generally amusing for everyone watching. Later in the evening the dance floor is handed over to the guests for an hour or so of disco dancing.

Village tours

Most Mediterranean resorts have lost their traditional ways of life as tourism has developed, so a village tour is the perfect way to see how the vast majority of Turks away from the cities and the coastal strip live. The Taurus Mountains running inland from the Mediterranean coast have some wonderful rural settlements where life continues almost as it has done for the last few thousand years – with the rhythm of the seasons. Worth a visit to see a different way of life.

⬧ *A typical* gület

Perge

The most complete ancient city so far discovered in the Turkish Mediterranean, the centre of Perge has been well excavated to reveal city streets, the remains of temples, shops and houses, and even a sophisticated communal air-conditioning system. The outskirts of the ancient site retain their allusive mystery, being shrouded in grasses and farmland.

Perge, founded around 1000 BC, was populated by the Pamphylians, who settled in the region and thrived on trade. It expanded under the Romans but declined under the Byzantines and Seljuks, and was finally abandoned before the end of the first millennium AD.

◓ *The red-stone Hellenistic Gate with remains of round towers*

Archaeologists believe that much of the site remained intact until as recently as the beginning of the Republic of Turkey in the 1920s, when a building boom brought local people to trawl the site for stone they could use for their houses.

ⓐ 29 km (18 miles) east of Antalya ⓒ 08.30–19.00 (May–Oct); 08.30–17.00 (Nov–Apr) ⓘ Admission charge

SITE TOUR

Theatre
Although not quite as impressive as Aspendos (see page 62), Perge's 2nd-century theatre is renowned for the fine friezes that adorned the stage wall – panels and theatre statues are on display in the Archaeological Museum in Antalya (see page 28). The theatre is usually closed due to archaeological excavations.

Stadium
This huge sporting arena, which is 234 m (256 yds) by 34 m (37 yds), with seating for 12,000 spectators, is the best example of its kind in the Mediterranean. The arcades under the terraces are believed to have housed shops and storage units.

Tomb of Plancia Magna
City records tell us that Plancia Magna was a great benefactress to the city, giving money for many public statues. Her tomb sits just outside the city gates beyond the ticket office. You can find a statue of her in the Archaeological Museum at Antalya (see page 27).

City gates
There are two gates to the city. The Roman Gate is a simple entrance way, but the earlier Hellenistic Gate is the most prominent building at Perge. In a city of marble the gate is built of red stone and is made up of two round towers (now half ruined) fronting a horseshoe-shaped atrium. In the Roman period this gate was decorated with statues

of the gods, but these are all now on display in the Antalya Archaeological Museum.

Roman baths

The impressive Roman baths complex is a good example of its kind. You can explore the *frigidarium* (cold room), *tepidarium* (warm room) and *caldarium* (hot room). Romans would move from one to the other to get the most beneficial treatment.

Roman *agora*

Across from the baths is the late-Roman *agora* (public open space), dating from the 4th century ad and constructed on a perfect square area measuring 75 sq m (89 sq yds).

Colonnaded street

The main thoroughfare of the city, this wide marble lane was lined with Ionic columns and was cooled and freshened by a sophisticated water feature. A monumental fountain at the head of the street some thousand metres (1,100 yds) to the north fed a metre-high (3 ft) marble channel, running along the centre of the street all the way down to the square behind the Hellenistic Gate, with cold water that cooled the surrounding air. Halfway along, there is a marble bridge to allow traffic to cross from one side of the street to the other. Shops flanked both sides of the street. Each has a mosaic floor, and some floors are still in good condition. Today, local ladies spread their handmade lace and other souvenirs all along the colonnaded street – echoing the past.

Exploring the unexcavated areas

Once you leave the well-excavated colonnaded way you find yourself among wild tussock grasses. There are still buildings to explore, including an acropolis area, a necropolis and vestiges of the Roman walls that once surrounded the city.

⬤ *Main colonnaded street in Perge*

Aspendos

The theatre at the city of Aspendos is the most impressive single ancient monument along the Mediterranean coast.

Yet the city of Aspendos played a relatively minor role in ancient history. During Roman times it made its living from panning salt, but the site has had a long life because it was not finally abandoned until the 18th century. Of course, many of the monumental buildings were left to fall into disrepair long before this, and the same was true of the theatre – which was built during the reign of Roman Emperor Marcus Aurelius (AD 161–80). When Turkish President Kemal Atatürk visited Aspendos in the 1920s, he ordered that the theatre should be renovated and preserved for the nation.

ⓐ 54 km (33½ miles) east of Antalya **ⓛ** 08.30–19.00 (Apr–Oct); 08.30–17.00 (Nov–Mar) **ⓘ** Admission charge

Around the theatre you may be followed by touts selling 'Roman' coins. These are not genuine but copies of real coins, and make an unusual souvenir – provided you don't pay the 'very special' initial price asked by the touts.

SITE TOUR

Theatre

This is one place where you could have stepped back in time. The theatre is just as it would have looked for Roman audiences and the bustle of your fellow visitors here gives an atmosphere of an audience arriving to take their seats for a performance. Built into a hillside in the classic Roman style (semicircular with a huge stage wall), the theatre seating area, or *cavea*, has 40 rows of seats and can accommodate an audience of over 15,000 people. Topping the *cavea* there is an ornate vaulted gallery and upper walkway, or *ambulacrum*, from where you can look down on the whole structure.

The stage wall was used in Roman times to support stage scenery such as huge painted theatre backdrops. It once had monumental statuary in each of the niches, but today these are empty and some of the statues are on display in the Archaeological Museum in Antalya (see page 27).

Aspendos Opera and Ballet Festival The highlight of the arts calendar in the Mediterranean region, this festival is held in the theatre each June and features Turkish and foreign companies performing classic and experimental opera and ballet. It is a majestic sight when the theatre stage is dressed and the orchestra breaks the silence of the balmy evening – truly an unforgettable experience. Tickets are on sale at the theatre or in Antalya (see page 25). Ask at the tourist office because there is no permanent ticket office.

Legend of Aspendos Theatre A local legend states that the ruler of the city decreed that his daughter would be married to the man who could build the most beautiful and useful building for the city. Two men took up the challenge; one constructed the theatre, the other the aqueduct. The citizens could not decide who should take the prize and the king offered to share his daughter by cutting her in two. The builder of the theatre pulled out of the agreement, whereupon he was offered her hand.

The view For the best overall view of the interior, walk up the hill behind the theatre and you can look down into the whole structure. There are several dirt paths but they are steep in places so take care.

The city
Aspendos city has not been excavated and the remains of its once-great buildings lie floundering in the surrounding farmland. The most obvious are the huge *nymphaeum* (ornate façade of a public fountain) and early Christian basilica. Look out also for long sections of the aqueduct that brought fresh water to the city from the hills in the distance (a total of 15 km, or 9½ miles, was originally built).

Rafting in the Köprülü Canyon

This is just about as energetic as you can get along the Turkish coast.
Köprülü rafting is world famous, but the rapids are not really difficult –
if you are a rafting novice, this is the perfect place to start. There is
enough white water to get your adrenalin rushing, but lots of quiet
spells in between for you to get your breath back and take in the
wonderful views.

⬥ Rafting in the Köprülü Canyon is for beginners and experts alike

THINGS TO SEE & DO

Rafts

The large rafts can take around 15 people so they're perfect for a group. You get a guide who shows you the basics, and you are kitted out with safety gear. There is a bit of singing to get you in the party mood, before it's 'paddles at the ready'.

Just after you set off you come to the first set of rapids, so watch out. This is where the photographers stand to get your souvenir photograph – usually a great view of the shocked look on your face – so smile through the terror.

Medraft This is the longest-established rafting company.
Ⓐ Hüseyin Kuzu Apt 14/3, Portakal Çiçeği Bl, Yesilbahçe Mah, Antalya Ⓣ 0242 312 5770 Ⓦ www.medraft.com ❶ Children under six are not allowed to ride for safety reasons

Kayaks

If the communal raft is not for you, you can hire one- and two-person kayaks and take the river at your own pace. Guided groups are great for beginners and novices because you have an experienced kayaker with you all the way.

Köprülü Canyon area

Upriver of the rafting base, the river snakes down from the foothills of the Taurus Mountains through a canyon, now protected as Köprülü Kanyon Milli Parkı (Köprülü Canyon National Park). You can explore this area on several footpaths.

All this excitement can really build up an appetite, so you'll be glad when it's lunchtime. At the canyon, there is a good choice of restaurants where you can enjoy a simple feast of barbecued meats and fresh trout with salads, followed by fruit, to replenish the energy levels.

Termessos & the Karain Cave

Still some way off the beaten tourist track, these two attractions, featuring some of Turkey's finest landscapes and a huge slice of ancient history, make a worthy day trip from the west of the region (Kemer, Antalya and Belek/Lara Beach).

There are few restaurants on your route so this trip provides the perfect chance to enjoy a picnic in the hills. There is lots of fresh fruit and vegetables plus delicious roast chicken and fresh bread in the local markets, or you can head to the huge hypermarket in the Migros Shopping Centre in Antalya.

You need to head inland towards Burdur before turning left towards Korkuteli after about 10 km (6 miles). The entrance to the Termessos site is on the left after about 15 km (9½ miles). It is also signposted Güllük Dağı Milli Parkı (Güllük Mountain National Park). From the ticket office the approach road leads another 9 km (5½ miles) through some wonderful Mediterranean scenery to the small car park at the base of the site.

ⓐ 34 km (21 miles) northwest of Antalya ⓑ 08.30–19.00 (Apr–Oct); 08.30–17.00 (Nov–Mar) ⓘ Admission charge; there are a few picnic tables close to the Termessos ticket office, which also has a small museum with a few finds and botanical information about the park. It can be worth having lunch before moving on.

TERMESSOS

The most dramatically sited ancient city along the Turkish coast, the ruins of ancient Termessos sit 1,000 m (3,281 ft) high in Güllük Dağı (Güllük Mountain Range), among granite crags and dense pine forest with magnificent views down to the coast in the south. Even in ancient times, Termessos was hard to reach, and so well sited for defensive purposes that even Alexander the Great could not conquer it. Termessos was built and populated by the Pisidians, who came from the central Anatolian plains. The remote location and impressive defences were two of the reasons why Alexander could not take the city during his campaign in 333 BC; another was the population, who spent the next couple of hundred years attacking the cities of the Lycian coast. Later they made a living extracting customs money from traders who had to take this route through the mountains from the coast to central Turkey. They also signed an accord with the Romans that allowed them to keep their independence within the empire. The city was abandoned after an earthquake in the 3rd century AD and never resettled. Termessos has never been excavated, and its remains are only kept clear of vegetation by the constant stream of visitors, but do take care because there are no fences or other safety precautions at the site.

SITE TOUR

Lower town

From the car park, you can examine the monumental Hadrian's Gate before beginning to climb uphill along the steep King's Road – which really sorts out the fit from the unfit. This was the main access way into the city and leads through two separate fortified walls.

Acropolis Plateau

Once through the walls you reach the first plateau (after about 20 minutes' walking), which was effectively the centre of the city. Set among huge granite boulders, the buildings do not have the fine details of Perge (see page 58), but display a more rugged, handsome strength. The gymnasium and baths complex are well preserved; there is a large mausoleum, a small stadium (sports activities were important to the ancient city) and the remains of several temples.

Theatre

Termessos theatre has the most impressive setting. Nestled in a rocky bowl, the *cavea*, or seating area, is not well preserved, but there is a breathtaking natural backdrop of the Mediterranean coastline, 1,000 m (1,100 yds) below.

Tomb of Alcatus

Alcatus was a leader of the Pisidians who defied the Greeks and committed suicide instead of being taken prisoner. This tomb has not been proved to be his, but the magnificent carved reliefs depicting a warrior on horseback date from around the time of his death in the early 3rd century BC and would be a fitting tribute to such an important man.

Necropolis

This is a remarkable collection of tombs and sarcophagi dating from late in the city's history (1st–3rd century AD). A lookout tower is set at the highest point in the city. From here you can get excellent panoramic long-distance views of the coast from near Kemer to Antalya and beyond to the east.

KARAIN CAVE

The earliest Turks lived in this complex of caves set 65 m (213 ft) above sea level, in cliffs flanking a fertile valley to the north of Antalya. This is one of the richest Palaeolithic sites in the world, with 11 m (36 ft) of chronological remains allowing archaeologists to piece together the history of the region from c 300,000 BC, when hippos, rhinos and elephants roamed free, to the present day.

The first humans came here 50,000 years ago and found it easy to hunt game and find fruit. Finds including tools and flints have helped to add a great deal to scientists' knowledge of our ancient relatives. The small museum has bones from ancient animals, including rhinos, hippos and smaller game that was obviously hunted by our early ancestors. The caves are a steep 20-minute hike up into the valley. There is a turning to Karain just outside the entrance to the Güllük Mountain National Park. From here it is 12 km (7½ miles) to the Karain Cave. After the initial turning the road splits but comes back together again about 4 km (2½ miles) further on.

ⓐ 42 km (26 miles) northwest of Antalya ● 08.30–18.00
❶ Admission charge

⬤ *The Roman amphitheatre at Termessos*

Myra (modern Demre/Kale)

The site at ancient Myra allows you to get up close to some of the best Lycian carved stone tombs in Turkey. The modern town of Kale (also known locally as Demre) close to the site has been a pilgrimage centre for many centuries because it is the birthplace of St Nicholas – Santa Claus or, as he is known in Turkey, Baba Noel.

THE SITE

Dating back to the 5th century BC, Myra was one of the most important cities of the ancient Lycian people, supplying a form of incense to the expanding Greek and Roman world. The city was finally abandoned after earthquake damage and much of it remains to be excavated. Today, there are three main areas to explore.

🚍 120 km (74½ miles) southwest of Antalya, 2 km (1¼ miles) north of Kale/Demre centre 🕓 08.30–19.30 (Apr–Oct); 08.30–17.00 (Nov–Mar) ❶ Admission charge

SITE TOUR

Sea Necropolis

This main collection of tombs is carved at eye level into the sheer cliff face. The tombs were carved to imitate the house of the subject during life, with an ornate door marking the entrance. You can get up close to the carvings to study the detail but you cannot go inside.

Theatre

Next to the tombs is a well-preserved theatre, one of the smallest at a major site. The entrance galleries and stairs used by Roman audiences are still pretty much intact, so you can climb them and imagine you are going to take your seat for an ancient play. There are good views towards the sea from the vaulted upper walkway. The decorative friezes of theatrical muse masks that once framed the stage now lie scattered across the site.

⬛ *The carved tombs of the Sea Necropolis at Myra*

⬥ *Roman theatre at Myra*

River Necropolis

A less-visited group of tombs can be found to the right of the theatre, a ten-minute walk from the main road through farmland. Known as the River Necropolis because it faces the river (usually dried up in summer), the most important tomb here is known as the 'Painted Tomb'. When it was first discovered by explorers in the 1840s the tomb was covered in bright pigment, but this has since disappeared. Even so, the reliefs depicting a Lycian family group are still impressive.

Noel Baba Kilisesi (The Church of St Nicholas)

Noel Baba Kilesi is a church which is associated with St Nicholas. It was built in the 8th century to house the body of the saint, although this was later lost during a pirate raid in the 11th century.

It is an excellent and attractive example of the Byzantine or Romanesque style of architecture. Decorated with beautiful inlaid patterned floors featuring rare and expensive stones and marbles, the church is also worth visiting for its wall frescoes, the best of which can be seen close to the entrance.

The tomb said to be that of St Nicholas can be found in the southern aisle, although this is actually of a later date. However, there is another tomb of the correct date that is now on display in the Archaeological Museum in Antalya (see page 27).

ⓐ 120 km (74½ miles) southwest of Antalya; in the town centre
🕒 08.30–19.00 (Apr–Oct); 08.30–17.00 (Nov–Mar) ❶ Admission charge

HOW PIOUS ST NICHOLAS BECAME JOLLY SANTA CLAUS

Christianity expanded quickly through the region after the 3rd century AD, and in the 4th century Myra became a bishopric. The first man to get the job was a local man, Nicholas, and he was said to have performed a number of miracles during his lifetime, including bringing several children back from the dead. He was made into a saint after his death.

The miracles St Nicholas performed made him the only sensible candidate for Patron Saint of Children, and 6 December was chosen as his saint's day. Over the centuries, in northern Europe and later in the United States, this religious St Nicholas gradually evolved into the jovial figure we know today, who wears his beard and robes because of the snowy December weather of the north.

Kekova boat trip

The coastal shallows of Kekova Sound in southeast Lycia make one of the most beautiful and popular trips along this part of the coast. Kekova Island shelters crystal-clear waters and numerous rocky islets. The vista is topped off by the jagged, arid Lycian peaks just inland.

Until recently, this idyllic corner of the Turkish coast was the exclusive preserve of 'yachties' who could lay anchor in one of the many remote coves seemingly hundreds of kilometres away from the rest of the world. Today, the pleasures of the area can be enjoyed by everyone for a lot less than the cost of a yacht charter – and with lunch included in the package. 🕐 Boat trips daily (weather permitting in winter) ❶ Admission charge (plus a charge for entering the castle)

The further you travel in a boat, the less time you'll have at Kekova, so you may not experience all the activities discussed below. The itinerary here assumes that you have sailed from the closest port, Üçağız, about 150 km (93 miles) west of Antalya. There are also cruises lasting several days from Antalya, which include Kekova on their itinerary.

THINGS TO SEE & DO

Kekova Island

Kekova Island lies only a few hundred metres offshore and only became an island when the level of the Mediterranean rose in the early part of the first millennium. As the water flooded in, it swallowed the ancient city that thrived here. The boat sails in to view what remains of Batıkkent (the 'sunken city'), but archaeologists haven't yet identified which city it actually was.

The island is protected as an ancient site so no one is allowed to set foot on it, but your boat will get in close to shore and you can get good views of the remains of numerous stone buildings clinging to the hillside, and the ancient harbour just below the waterline. Under the water are the remains of yet more buildings, and the sea bed is dotted with ancient pottery amphorae lying where they fell many hundreds of years ago.

The necropolis of Teimiussa

On the inland shoreline are the remains of ancient Teimiussa, half-submerged in water and half-choked by the fertile mud that now helps make this part of Turkey the capital of fruit and vegetable production. Look out particularly for several excellent Lycian tombs rising out of the water, supported on their stone pillars.

Kaleköy

Kaleköy (the ancient site of Simena) is one of the prettiest and most authentic, untouched villages along the Turkish coast, and the view as you approach from the water makes a perfect picture, with a rash of traditional whitewashed houses climbing up the hillside, crowned by a sturdy fortress (see below).

Once your boat has moored at one of the numerous rustic wooden jetties, you are free to explore the narrow winding alleyways. The settlement is a fascinating mixture of living community and tourist town. Most of the houses are family homes and chickens roam free throughout the village, scattering noisily as you approach. The older women sit in their doorways crocheting or making the lace that is on sale everywhere; children offer fruit or small trinkets, while carpet shops simply hang their wares off balconies or over walls.

The Fortress of the Knights of St John

Tours usually include a visit to this fortress, built by the Knights of St John and offering wonderful high-level views over the sound and down over the town. It's one of their smaller outposts, but still a beautiful example of crusader architecture.

🕐 24 hours ❶ Admission charge when guardian is on duty

Swimming

After your explorations, you will be allowed time for swimming and snorkelling. Watch out for the spiny sea urchins that breed in the shallows here. If you step on them, the spines break off in your foot and can become infected.

Olymbos & Chimaera

Most easily reached from the western Mediterranean resorts but worth the trip from the others, the narrow coastal strip south of Kemer is hemmed in against the sea by high, pine-clad cliffs, and even in the late 1990s it was still remote from the rest of Turkey. It was regarded as a hippy or backpacker destination with simple accommodation in tree houses and cabins for the few who ventured here – almost like a Turkish version of the book *The Beach*. Today, the bay makes a popular boat trip from around the coast, and the newly upgraded road has improved access for cars.

OLYMBOS (OLYMPOS)
Olymbos beach

One of the finest on the stretch of coast that includes the good beaches of Kemer and Beldibi, Olymbos is particularly beautiful because it is still backed by lush vegetation, not concrete hotels. There are a few cafés under the pines and a village centre at Çıralı, but no high-rise buildings to spoil the natural view. It is especially dramatic against the mountainous backdrop only a few hundred metres inland.

Olymbos site

Ancient Olymbos occupied a spectacular site by a natural spring close to the beach. Named after nearby Mount Olymbos – now Tahtalı Dağ – it was an important Lycian town dating from around 200 BC. The chief god of the town was Hephaistos (known to the Romans as Vulcan), patron of fire and of blacksmiths. This was obviously a direct result of the natural flames of Chimaera close by (see opposite). The site continued to be occupied after the fall of Rome and was an important port for the Byzantines and the Genoese between the 7th and 14th centuries.

Today, the unexcavated site is rather a jumble in the verdant vegetation. The Byzantine and Genoese walls and fortifications at the seaward end of the site are among the most obvious structures.

The city was a target for pirates throughout the first millennium so the fortifications were very necessary.

Just below the harbour fortifications are the Harbour Tombs, two Lycian funerary monuments, one of which has had its inscription translated into English. Explore further inland on the well-worn paths to find scant remains of warehouses, villas and a theatre.

Until recently, the fresh water that surrounds and sometimes submerges the site was a haven for wildlife such as frogs, birds and insects, but since it has become more popular and the water quality has been spoilt by sun lotions and litter left by visitors who should know better, they have all but disappeared.

🅐 75 km (47 miles) southwest of Antalya 🕐 08.30–19.00 (Apr–Oct); 08.30–17.00 (Nov–Mar) ❶ Admission charge

CHIMAERA

The natural flames rising out of the rocks on Tahtalı Dağ peak have been seen since ancient times. Then, sailors thought that they were the breath of the chimaera – the monster with a lion's front, a goat's rear and a dragon's tail. The Turks call the flames *yanartaş*, or 'burning rock'. Greek myth tells us that the chimaera was killed when Bellerophon dropped molten lead into its mouth, but the flames still burn – although they have been a little diminished over the centuries and are certainly not visible from offshore any more.

It is a 20-minute walk into the hills from the car park at the ticket office, but if you have arrived on a boat trip you should allow an hour to walk from Çıralı village (a three-hour round trip with time to view the flames). Most of the flames do not rise much above calf height and many of them are very transparent, so take care not to get burnt as you clamber over the rocks.

🅐 75 km (47 miles) southwest of Antalya 🕐 24 hours – a ticket office is staffed 08.30–19.00 (Apr–Oct); 08.30–17.00 (Nov–Mar) ❶ There is an admission charge when the ticket office is open

Pamukkale

Pamukkale (Pamuk-alay) means 'cotton castle' in Turkish, and it is a most appropriate name. This huge natural travertine fountain is one of the country's most famous attractions and one of its most beautiful and spectacular landscapes. Terraces of shallow limestone pools the shape of oyster shells cling to the hillside like a giant, stepped pool against the blue sky. From a distance it looks like piles of raw cotton; close up, the limestone is brilliant white and its edges glitter like diamonds – so don't forget your sunglasses! It's an overnight trip inland from the Mediterranean coast, but well worth a visit.

SITE TOUR

The Travertine Cascades
Several storeys of pure white shallow bowls are filled with azure-blue waters shimmering in the sunshine. ⓐ 265 km (165 miles) northwest of Antalya ⓛ 24 hours – a ticket office is staffed during daylight hours ⓘ Admission fee charged when ticket office is staffed

⬥ *The Travertine Cascades in Pamukkale*

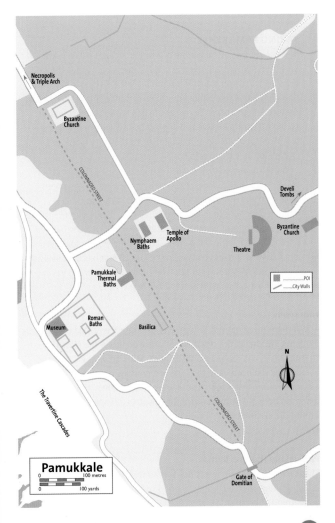

Necropolis
& Triple Arch

Byzantine
Church

COLONNADED STREET

Develi
Tombs

Nymphaem
Baths

Temple of
Apollo

Byzantine
Church

Theatre

Pamukkale
Thermal
Baths

POI

City Walls

Museum

Roman
Baths

Basilica

N

The Travertine Cascades

COLONNADED STREET

Pamukkale

| 0 | | 100 metres |
| 0 | | 100 yards |

Gate of
Domitian

SAVING PAMUKKALE

In the early days, there was no protection for Pamukkale's delicate environment. People broke the sides of the pools as they climbed over them and sun oils from swimmers left a residue in the water that discoloured the white limestone. To add to this, several hotels that were built above the cascade began to use water from the spring for their own swimming pools, so it wasn't reaching the limestone pools to repair the damage. By the early 1990s 'cotton castle' was in real danger.

In the mid-1990s, the Turkish authorities instigated an action plan to save the Cascades. The hotels on the plateau have been bulldozed and the waters are being trained over the most damaged sections to make them white once again, a bit like the now-popular teeth-whitening process. People have been banned from bathing in or walking on the pools. There is a footpath you can follow as long as you take your shoes off, but it is a bit painful for soft feet! All these changes have made a huge difference, and the total area of white limestone has begun to expand again.

Hierapolis

The Romans loved natural springs. They thought they could cure various ailments. Hierapolis, the city they built here on top of the plateau next to Pamukkale, was really a giant spa town. Walk down the Cardo, the colonnaded main street, to the Gate of Domitian, or explore the Necropolis (cemetery), with its collection of more than 1,200 tombs and giant sarcophagi. The **museum** on site displays a range of items found during the excavation.

ℹ️ Extra ticket charge

Pamukkale Thermal Baths

These baths have been open since Roman times and the modern buildings have been built directly on top of the ancient ones. While you are bathing, you can sit on fallen Roman columns that lie just under the surface of the water. The warm springs are said to be good for arthritis, stress and a long list of other ailments – although most people just come for the fun of swimming there. Even if you do not want to get wet (extra charge), come and have a look at the pools.

🕐 09.00–20.00

🔺 *Pamukkale town at the foot of the hot springs*

Ephesus

The largest and most complete ancient city in the eastern Mediterranean, Ephesus is a must-see site. The exceptionally well-preserved buildings, with little touches that bring the citizens to life, allow us to step back in time to the late Roman era, when this was the capital of Asia Minor. It's a long trip from the Mediterranean region, over 500 km (310 miles) west of Antalya, and at least one overnight stay is necessary. Tours often include visits to Pamukkale and other sites.

HISTORY

Founded in the 11th century BC, Ephesus became an important and rich city because it was the centre of worship for the goddess of fertility, Artemis. The temple here was one of the Seven Wonders of the Ancient World and attracted pilgrims from around ancient Greece.

In Roman times, the city was capital of Asia Minor with a population of over 250,000. It was a trading and banking city of immense wealth and was one of the most advanced cities in the empire, with both flushing communal latrines and street lighting.

It was an important Christian city with a close association with St Paul of Tarsus and was populated until the 11th century AD. The last few hundred years brought serious problems when its port on the River Cayster began to silt up. Eventually it was cut off from the sea completely, making trade impossible. The city was then abandoned.

SITE TOUR

Arcadian Way

One of the first Roman streets to get municipal lighting (in the 5th century AD), Arcadian Way led from the theatre to the port. The widest avenue in the city, much of it is now off limits, but it is possible to stand at the top (in front of the theatre) and look towards what would have been the warehouse district and the waterfront during Roman times.

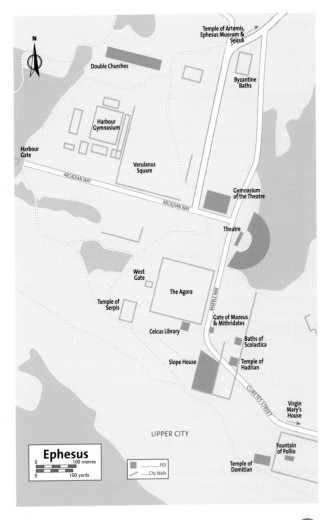

N

Temple of Artemis,
Ephesus Museum &
Selçuk

Double Churches

Byzantine
Baths

Harbour
Gymnasium

Harbour
Gate

Verulanus
Square

ARCADIAN WAY

ARCADIAN WAY

Gymnasium
of the Theatre

Theatre

West
Gate

The Agora

Temple of
Serpis

MARBLE WAY

Gate of Mazeus
& Mithridates

Celcus Library

Baths of
Scolastica

Slope House

Temple of
Hadrian

CURETES STREET

Virgin
Mary's
House

UPPER CITY

Fountain
of Pollio

Ephesus

0   100 metres

0   100 yards

Temple of
Domitian

POI

City Walls

Upper City

A plateau at the top of the hill is the least exciting part of the city. Around the wide space that was once the Upper Agora, you will be able to explore the administrative headquarters, a small *odeon* (theatre) and the remains of a thermal spa. The best part of the upper city is the view down over the rest of Ephesus. From the small square in front of the Monument of Memmius, which was erected in homage to the citizens of the city, you get a most breathtaking view down Curetes Street, one of the most photographed vistas in Turkey. Beyond, look out over the flat area where there is a modern airfield. This used to be the port for the ancient city. Take some time to search for the coast in the distance. This is how far the sea has receded since Roman times and shows why the city was doomed; with no way to transport goods overland, it couldn't function.

Curetes Street

The major arterial route linking the upper city with the port, Curetes Street had shops selling goods from around the empire, along with a number of important temples. These include the Temple of Hadrian (built *c* AD 117–38), with its distinctive double archway of fine Corinthian columns and an elaborate frieze dedicated to the goddess Tyche.

Slope House

On each side of Curetes Street, the residential quarters of Ephesus lie on the terraced hillside, reached by narrow alleyways. These were the houses of the rich, and one three-storey residence, Yamaç Evleri or Slope House, has undergone a thorough excavation to offer a glimpse of the Roman lifestyle and interior design. The spacious rooms are decorated with incredible original mosaic floors and wall frescoes that were the height of fashion.

❶ Extra admission charge, but it is worth it

Gate of Mazeus and Mithridates

Linking the library and the neighbouring *agora*, the Gate of Mazeus and Mithridates was commissioned by two slaves freed by the Emperor

Augustus, who went on to become leading citizens of the city. It is built in the style of a triumphal arch.

Celcus Library

At the bottom of Curetes Street, the library is one of the focal points of the city. Erected in AD 117 as a memorial to Tiberius Julius Celsus by his son, it has a grandiose two-storey façade decorated with fluted columns and statues depicting The Four Virtues: Goodness (*Arete*), Thought (*Ennoia*), Knowledge (*Episteme*) and Wisdom (*Sophia*). The library once held 12,000 scrolls and was considered a great centre of learning.

Baths of Scolastica

The baths were one of the social centres of the city, a place where men got together to do business deals, debate politics or simply gossip. These were built by a rich woman named Scolastica in the 1st century AD. They're located in the heart of the city almost opposite the Celcus Library, and you can still see the hot room and cold room.

Theatre

One of the prettiest and most complete Roman theatres, Ephesus theatre is still used during the important Ephesus Festival of Culture and Art each May. During Roman times, 24,000 people would cram the stands to enjoy drama and comedy, and to see gladiatorial and animal fights. It was also the scene of many of St Paul's evangelical speeches. He was cornered here by angry Ephesians when he criticised their beloved Artemis, but managed to escape.

Marble Way

Linking Curetes Street with Arcadian Way, the short Marble Way has a couple of interesting things to see. Notice how the marble of the road surface has been worn away by the passing of hundreds of thousands of cart wheels. No doubt these carts were heavily laden with goods for market. There is also an advertisement for a brothel etched in a stone of the road, pointing the way to the entrance close by.

Temple of Artemis

A kilometre (½ mile) away from the city is the Temple of Artemis or Artemision, the most important temple to Artemis in the ancient world. A mammoth building, it houses a life-size gold statue to the goddess. It was so impressive that it was known as one of the Seven Wonders of the Ancient World, but today it is a shadow of its former self. The Goths destroyed the site in AD 262 and much of the stone was later recycled – only the main temple platform and a couple of lonely columns remain. Although the statue has never been found, there are several stone and marble statues of her in the Ephesus Museum at Selçuk (see below).

Ephesus Museum

If you visit the site of Ephesus, you must also visit the Ephesus Museum in the nearby town of Selçuk (Seljuk). This is where the best of the artefacts found at the site are on display.

The museum is not too big and overwhelming and includes the re-creation of a Roman room excavated at the site, complete with furniture and a small domestic shrine. The range of everyday objects on display is impressive, from hairpins to leather sandals. More precious objects include gold filigree jewellery and fine Samian tableware.

Several rooms display monumental statuary and friezes that decorated temples and public buildings, as well as the Hall of the Emperors, where statues and busts of many Roman leaders have been brought together.

ⓐ 129 km (80 miles) north of Marmaris. Agora Çarşısı, Selçuk
🕓 08.30–12.00 & 13.00–19.00 ❶ Admission charge

Cappadocia

It is a day's journey from the Mediterranean coast inland to Cappadocia and you should spend at least a night in the area (accommodation is often included in the price). This is one of Turkey's most fascinating regions for its spectacular natural landscapes, its religious treasures and its modern-day rural lifestyles.

A total contrast to the verdant pine forests and farmland of the coast, at first Cappadocia seems like a vast expanse of white stone devoid of any life. In fact, it is a very fertile region famed for its wine and, in years gone past, for its horses. Methods of farming have not changed much for generations because the narrow valleys that shelter the fields do not allow for mass production. Donkeys and mules are used as a matter of course here, rather than trucks or tractors. Families live

⬤ *Rock homes cut into the volcanic tufa at Cappadocia*

comfortably in their small, rock-cut homes. Further caves provide storage rooms and shelter for livestock.

During the Byzantine era (4th–11th centuries AD), the region had a thriving Christian community with several important monasteries. The concentration of early churches and their wall paintings (frescoes) represents one of the most important collections of religious art and architecture in the world.

HISTORY

Cappadocia has been swept up in the east-to-west movement of the great empires over the last 4,000 years. It was the centre of the Hittite Empire from c 1800 to 1200 BC before the Persians became overlords. Then the Romans arrived and built a regional capital, Caesarea, at what is now the town of Kayseri.

Following the division of the Roman Empire in the 4th century, Cappadocia became part of the Christian Byzantine Empire with its capital at Constantinople (now Istanbul). The Seljuk Muslims arrived from the east during the 12th century, followed by the Ottomans in the 15th century, but the region became a backwater under Islam.

In 1907, a French priest rediscovered the early churches during an expedition through the Turkish hinterland, but it was not until the late 1980s that Cappadocia became part of the established tourist trail.

THE CHRISTIAN ERA

St Paul introduced Christianity to Cappadocia as early as the first century AD when he passed through here on his evangelical journeys. The community grew quietly away from the gaze of Pagan Rome, then flourished when Christianity was declared the legal religion of the empire. As time passed, this region was on the northeast outskirts of safe Christian territory and was prone to Arab raids from the east – that is the reason why so many churches were hidden from view in narrow and remote valleys.

HOW THE LANDSCAPE WAS CREATED

The whole Cappadocia region used to be volcanic and is covered with a layer of soft grey-white volcanic rock called tufa. It is easily worn away by rain and wind, and over the centuries these forces have fashioned the beautiful and surreal shapes, revealing layers of differing colours and the rounded curves and towers seen all across the region.

FAIRY CHIMNEYS

Most famous of the Cappadocian features are the 'fairy chimneys'. These are created when a layer of hard rock sits on top of a layer of tufa. Over time rain gets into the cracks of the harder rock and washes away the tufa below, except for that situated directly underneath the hard rock. Eventually, as more tufa gets washed away, all that is left is a tall column with a rock hat on top.

THINGS TO SEE & DO

Avanos

Set on the Red River, Avanos is famed for the distinctive red pottery made from the clay of the surrounding hills that has been around since Hittite times. The old town with its Ottoman and Greek mansions is a splendid place for a stroll and some shopping.
ⓐ 12 km (7¹/₂ miles) north of Göreme

Balloon ride

A hot-air balloon ride allows the best views of the marvellous shapes and contours of the unique landscape. You depart at dawn (weather permitting), and glide effortlessly along for around an hour or so before landing to enjoy a celebratory glass of bubbly with your breakfast.
Antalya Balloons This Austrian/Turkish joint venture offers hot-air balloon flights over Cappadocia, Aspendos and Belek.

Ⓐ Akdeniz Mahallesi Atif Zengin Cd 20, Belek ☎ 0242 715 1408/0533 220 8702 Ⓦ http://antalyaballoons.com/en

Derinkuyu

Cappadocia has a whole collection of underground settlements carved from the tufa to allow the local populations to live in safety from invading forces. These cities are thought to be much older than the rock-cut churches – perhaps even dating back to Hittite times.

The best-excavated of the cities is Derinkuyu, meaning 'deep well' in Turkish. Eight storeys have been studied so far – that is over 50 m (164 ft) underground – but archaeologists estimate that this is only a quarter of the whole city. Here, you can explore how the people lived their lives, with stables for livestock, kitchens, dining rooms and churches. Sophisticated ventilation brought fresh air in and let stale air and smoke escape, while the wells after which the town is now named provided a constant supply of water.

Ⓐ 40 km (25 miles) south of Göreme ⏱ 08.00–19.00 (July–Sept); 08.00–17.00 (Oct–Apr); 08.00–17.00 (May–June) ❶ Admission charge

Göreme Village

Göreme is a tourist town full of cafés and shops, set among the most beautiful and typical tufa landscapes. Just a short walk or drive out of the centre you can find people still living in their rock houses growing vines and keeping livestock in the sheltered valleys.

Göreme Open-Air Museum

This World Heritage Site now protects some of the finest treasures of Cappadocia, a cluster of over 30 rock-cut Byzantine churches and chapels that represents the development of religious art between the 4th and 11th centuries, and paints a picture of how the Christian community lived during its years of relative isolation. Whenever you visit, one or more of these churches will probably be closed for renovation because they are both precious and fragile. Each has something to offer, listed opposite are some of the highlights.

ⓐ 2 km (1¼ miles) north of Göreme ⓛ 08.30–17.30 (Apr–Oct); 08.30–17.00 (Nov–Mar) ❶ Admission charge

Elmalı Kilise (Apple Church) The most famous of the churches, Apple Church is decorated with stunning and colourful frescoes depicting Christ Pantocrator (enthroned) surrounded by angels. These 11th-century images are some of the latest in the museum and show a sophistication of imagery and development of artistic style. Look also for the simple red-ochre decoration added during the Iconoclastic period (the 8th and early 9th centuries), which was a time when decorating churches with images of the saints was frowned upon.

Yılanlı Kilise (Church of the Snakes) This church is renowned for its depiction of the early Byzantine saints. These include ruler Constantine and his mother St Helena holding the True Cross, St Onophrius, who lived as a hermit in the Egyptian desert and the martyr St Theodore, a Roman soldier who refused to renounce Christ and worship the pagan Roman gods.

Karanlık Kilise (Dark Church) The lack of light in this church preserved the vivid colour of the frescoes, and with a well-managed renovation programme in the 1990s these are now the pride of the collection. They also give the greatest indication of how the other churches would have looked in their heyday. One of the most dramatic frescoes to look out for is the Betrayal of Judas and Christ Crucified.
❶ Admission charge

New Church This church holds some of the best Christian frescoes in the Byzantine world, including 10th-century images depicting scenes from the life of Christ. These hark back to the early, pre-Iconoclastic era, but there is a new realism in the figures – shown by shading and layering in the paintings – displaying a development in style over the period. The most evocative scenes are the Descent from the Cross and Passion and Resurrection.

SHOPPING

Cappadocia is one of the best places in Turkey to buy a genuine antique or carpet. Although prices are not necessarily any cheaper than on the coast, there is a better choice and your souvenir will certainly be unique.

Uçhisar

The village is dominated by the Uçhisar rock castle, a massive 60 m (197 ft) dome of tufa that was once a living community. It is almost like a gigantic 3-D puzzle that you can actually climb into. Every centimetre of it has been carved to create living space and the views are spectacular. You can explore the cobbled streets of this farming community, complete with tethered donkeys and flocks of chickens and geese.

ⓐ 4 km (2¹/₂ miles) southwest of Göreme ⓑ 08.00–20.30
ⓘ Admission charge

Zelve Open-Air Museum

Originally a large Christian monastery, the carved rock complex in the three valleys that make up Zelve were inhabited as late as the 1950s. Several levels of rooms can be seen – you can climb the metal stairs to explore some sections – but there are very few fine frescoes here. The simple painted crosses in the chapels indicate that the complex was decorated during the Iconoclastic era.

ⓐ 8 km (5 miles) northeast of Göreme ⓑ 08.00–19.00 (Apr–Oct); 08.00–17.00 (Nov–Mar) ⓘ Admission charge

● *The astonishing castle in the rock at Uçhisar*

Selge

If you head further up into the hills beyond the Köprülü rafting base you pass into the Köprülü Canyon National Park (see page 65), an area of pine-clad granite peaks blanketed in wild scrub and herbs. Few tour buses find their way here, so although you are not far from the resorts, this is true natural Turkey. After 7 km (4½ miles) you reach a small village called Altınköy. Here, people are still making a living from farming, and the women sit in their doorways crocheting or making lace.

Scattered around the village are the remains of ancient Selge, once a city with a population of over 20,000 people. The site has not been excavated, but well-worn paths lead to the major buildings, which include a partly buried *agora* and atmospheric theatre.

If you need a guide, enquire in the village – one of the local men will show you around for a small fee.

ⓐ 55 km (34 miles) from the 400 coast road, 7 km (4½ miles) from rafting station **ⓒ** Informal ticket sales in village **ⓘ** Admission charge when ticket seller is in the area

---

ⓞ *Beautiful coloured-glass trinkets for sale*

LIFESTYLE
Mediterranean life

Food & drink

Turkish cuisine is considered to be one of the greatest in the world. For an excellent book on the subject, see *Turkish Cookery* by Sally Mustoe (Saqi Books). Though the days of the great Ottoman banquets are long gone, Turks still make meal times an event.

Freshness is the key to Turkish food – you need only look at the mountains of seasonal fruit and vegetables on sale in local markets or the seafood on ice at harbour-front restaurants for evidence of this. Dishes are generally cooked in olive oil, and a range of herbs and spices has traditionally been used to add flavour, but these are never overpowering.

WHEN TO EAT

Turks take a very relaxed approach to meal times. There will always be somewhere open no matter what time you get hungry, though you will find most atmosphere between 12.00 and 14.30 for lunch and between 19.00 and 22.00 for dinner, when other people head out to eat. Only the most formal restaurants close between lunch and dinner, and eateries of all kinds tend to stay open until the last client leaves.

In Turkey, food is usually served warm rather than hot, which usually means chips arrive soggy not crisp. If you want yours piping hot, tell the waiter when you order.

WHERE TO EAT

Choosing these different styles of eateries depends on your appetite:

Kahve A Turkish coffee house that does not serve food and is usually where men get together for a game of backgammon or a gossip.

Lokanta A casual, often family-owned restaurant serving a small range of home-cooked dishes. There will probably not be a printed menu, but it is normal to go into the kitchen to see what is being cooked. Point at what you want if the staff do not speak English.

Restoran A more formal restaurant than a *lokanta*. A *restoran* will have a printed menu with prices.

Kebapçı Specialises in grilled meats. They vary from pretty, family-owned establishments with outdoor terraces to small, urban kiosks.

Meyhane A bar- or pub-style place serving *meze* with drinks. These have traditionally been for males only, but in tourist areas women will also be welcomed.

Pideci These small snack bars serve Turkish pizza (see page 98).

Büfe A basic snack bar.

Pastane Turkish patisseries serving cakes and pastries.

WHAT TO EAT

Meze dishes or starters

Turks prefer to eat *meze* style. That is where several small dishes are served at once and shared by everyone around the table. Try eating *meze* style for a truly authentic experience, or order these dishes to have as a starter.

Cold options include *yaprak dolması* (stuffed vine leaves), fresh olives, *imam bayıldı* (slices of aubergine with tomatoes and onions in olive oil) and *cacık* (a refreshing dip of natural yoghurt and cucumber with a hint of mint). Warm *meze* dishes include *börek* (filo pastry squares filled with cheese and herbs) and *midye dolması* (stuffed mussels).

Because Turks eat *meze* style, you may find that if you order starters and main courses they will both arrive together. To avoid this, order only one course at a time.

Main courses

The most popular form of main course is grilled or barbecued meat, usually lamb, but you will also find some beef. It is grilled as chops or steak but also cubed and skewered for *şiş kebaps*, thinly sliced for *döner kebaps* or minced for *köfte* (meatballs) or *İskender kebap* (minced meat wrapped around a skewer). Meat is always fresh and is generally served cooked through, not pink in the middle or rare.

Fresh fish is plentiful and delicious. You will find it elaborately displayed on ice at restaurant entrances. It is, however, always the most expensive item on the menu. It is sold by weight, so you choose a fish and it will be weighed and priced for you, then cooked to your specifications. If you find the price beyond your budget, you get the chance to change your mind before it is too late.

You will normally find that your main meal comes with bread and salad and either rice or chips.

Snacks

Turkey has excellent pizza (*pide* or *lahmacun*), though it is lighter than the Italian variety and often served rolled up so you can eat it on the go. Equally delicious are *döner kebaps*, slivers of lamb wrapped with salad in pitta bread, and you can find these on almost every street corner. *Gözleme* are pancakes or crêpes with sweet or savoury fillings, while *semit* (bread rings sprinkled with sesame seeds) are perfect for stopping those afternoon hunger pangs.

Sweets

Turkish sweets and puddings are world renowned and make no apology for the amount of calories they contain. The most famous, *baklava* – layers of filo pastry soaked in butter, sprinkled with nuts then baked in honey syrup – is a work of art. Milk puddings are also popular, and are often delicious rich rice puddings evoking those we enjoyed as children. *Lokum* or Turkish delight (a jelly sweet traditionally flavoured with rose water, but you will find many fruit flavours today) makes a great accompaniment to Turkish coffee.

If all this really sounds a little over the top, most *lokantas* and *restorans* offer fresh melon or other seasonal fruit as a lighter but

TIPPING

Most *restorans* will add 10–15 per cent to your bill, but you should still leave a little something for the waiter. *Lokantas* will normally not add service to the bill. It is customary to leave 10–15 per cent. Leave small change on the table at bars and coffee houses.

equally delicious end to your meal. The sweet toothed will need to head to a specialist café for dessert. These are often very basic establishments with vinyl-topped tables and fluorescent lights, so they do not get points for romantic ambience, but they are full of authentic atmosphere.

International food

More and more 'international' food has become available in Turkey. This includes all-day English breakfasts if that's what you want, as well as other familiar items like pizzas and burgers. If you want to splash out, the large, upmarket hotels will have formal and expensive restaurants serving 'continental' menus with silver service.

Drinks

The usual array of fizzy soft drinks and international spirits is readily available, so you will certainly find something familiar during your trip. But why not try a particularly Turkish beverage? *Kahve*, or Turkish coffee, is strong but never harsh and served in small cups. Take it *sade* (no sugar), *az şekerli* (a little sugar) or *çok şekerli* (sweet), but never try to empty the cup because there are grounds in the bottom. *Çay* (tea) is served weak without milk in tulip-shaped glasses. Apple tea is a refreshing alternative. Another delicious non-alcoholic drink is *ayran*, a refreshing natural-yoghurt drink. Bottled water is also readily available (don't drink water from the tap).

Turkey produces some excellent wine. Look for the trade names Doluca and Kavaklıdere for quality and reliability. It also brews a good, clean-tasting Pilsen-type beer under the brand name Efes, but for something more potent try *rakı*, an anis-based spirit that is diluted with water. It is taken as both a before- or after-dinner drink, but, at a strength of 40 per cent, should always be taken in moderation.

Menu decoder

A FEW BASIC WORDS

Alabalık Freshwater trout

Aşure Sweet 'soup' of fruits, nuts, pulses and bulgar wheat

Balık Fish

Barbunya Red mullet

Beyti kebap Minced beef or lamb kebab wrapped in bread and served with tomato sauce and yoghurt

Bonfile Steak

Börek Savoury pastry usually with cheese filling but can be meat

Bülbül yuvası (swallow's nest) Shredded wheat in sugar syrup

Çay Tea

Çöp kebap Little chunks of meat roasted on a wooden skewer

Dolma Vine leaves stuffed with rice and herbs

Döner kebap Thin slices of grilled lamb sliced from a cone of meat

Ekmek Bread

Fasulye Haricot beans in tomato sauce

Fırında sütlaç Oven-baked rice pudding usually served cold

Gözleme A wafer-thin crêpe with sweet or savoury filling

Güllaç Flaky pastry and milk flavoured with nuts and rose water

Güveç Meat and/or vegetable stew, cooked in a clay pot

Hamsi Anchovy

Haydarı Yoghurt dip flavoured with garlic

İmam bayıldı Translated as 'the imam fainted' – a classic Ottoman dish of baked aubergine with tomatoes and onions served cold

İskender kebap Minced meat cooked around a skewer and served as wide strips of meat in yoghurt or tomato sauce

İstakoz Lobster

Kabak tatlısı Baked squash topped with clotted cream (*kaymak*)

Kahve Turkish coffee

Kalamar Squid

Karides Shrimp
Karışık ızgara Mixed grill of lamb meat
Karnıyarık Aubergines stuffed with minced lamb, currants and pine nuts then baked
Karpuz Watermelon
Kayısı Apricot
Kiraz Cherry
Kuzu Lamb
Lahmacun A wafer-thin pizza topped with tomato sauce and minced lamb
Levrek Sea bass
Maden suyu Mineral water
Manti Noodle dough ravioli parcels filled with meat
Menemen Stir-fried omelette with hot peppers and vegetables
Mercimek çorbası Lentil soup
Midye Mussel
Pastırma Dry-cured beef served thinly sliced
Pide Small, flat pizzas with a thin topping of minced lamb or cheese
Pilav Rice
Piliç Roast chicken
Pirzola Lamb chop
Piyaz Haricot beans in vinaigrette
Portakal Orange
Salata Salad
Şarap Wine
Sardalya Sardine
Sığır Beef
Şiş kebap Cubes of meat put on a skewer then grilled
Su Water
Süt Milk
Tarama Pink fish-roe dip
Tavuk Boiled chicken
Tel kadayıf Shredded wheat base smothered in honey syrup and chopped nuts
Turşu Pickled vegetables
Tuz Salt
Yayla çorbası Rice soup
Yoğurt çorbası Yoghurt soup

Shopping

There is something for everyone in Mediterranean Turkey, with a whole range of excellent souvenirs in all price brackets. You will be bombarded with designer rip-offs offering those must-have names at a fraction of the price back home. Many visitors take this opportunity to stock up on items by their favourite fashion house, which can be fun, but remember to check merchandise carefully, as quality varies from good to terrible.

Leather is also one of the top-ten buys for tourists. You will find a fantastic range of bags, belts and jackets. Again, designer names predominate but you can find traditional styles or have something made just for you.

Turkey is famous for its handicrafts and these include inlaid wooden items like small tables or chess sets, copper pots, rustic ceramics and pottery, onyx or Meerschaum pipes carved from a hard white clay found only in Turkey.

Gold and silver jewellery is also good value as items such as chains and bracelets are priced by weight. You can have things made at small jewellery workshops within a few days. Gold is usually 14-carat quality. Always check for the hallmark on gold and silver items.

The prize souvenir has to be the handmade Turkish carpet. These have been woven for centuries – each region has traditional patterns and colours. The best are made of silk, but most are wool.

Kilims are different to carpets because they have a flat weave rather than a pile. These are just as colourful but generally cheaper and they make great rugs and throws.

BROWSING

Browsing and window-shopping are not things the Turks do. When shopkeepers see you looking at their wares, they assume you have an interest in buying. Obviously, they would rather you buy from them than from the shop next door, so they will put a lot of effort into getting you to stop, look and try.

BARTERING

Bartering or bargaining is a fact of life in Turkey. It is not something that comes naturally to a shopper who is used to fixed prices, but that doesn't mean it is something to be nervous or worried about. If you are in the market to buy an expensive souvenir such as a leather jacket or a Turkish carpet, you will be paying well over the odds if you simply pay what the shopkeeper asks.

Here are some tips to make the bartering process more successful and enjoyable:

- To start with, act cool about the specific item you want. Look at several items and then perhaps tell the shopkeeper you want to look in other shops to compare goods.
- You will be offered a drink – Turkish tea or a soft drink – and it shows that you are more serious about buying if you accept.
- Your first offer should be around 50 per cent of what the shop owner asks, then increase your offer little by little. You will probably end up paying around 70 per cent of the original asking price, but early or late in the season it could be more.
- If you don't want to pay the price, just say so and walk away. The shop owner may call you back with a lower offer. Once you agree a price it is very bad manners to change your mind!
- You will get a better price if you pay in cash rather than with a credit card, and better still if you pay in pounds sterling or euros rather than in Turkish lira.

Children

Turkey is an ideal destination for children. The simple pleasures of guaranteed sunshine, excellent beaches and warm water to play in will keep them happy for hours. Add to this the child-friendly environment, where children are welcomed in restaurants and cafés, and it makes for a very relaxed holiday. Exuberance is not frowned upon here. Turks love children and allow them the freedom to enjoy their childhood.

That said, you will find fewer attractions specifically aimed at children than in many European destinations. There are no children's museums, few 'theme' parks and no games arcades. But the jet-skiing and water rides make up for that, as well as the chance to spot a wild dolphin or turtle during a boat trip.

TIPS FOR A CHILD-FRIENDLY TRIP

Turkish excursions can be heavy on history, and even the most enthusiastic adults can tire of this. Pace the sightseeing so you can alternate days of gazing at ancient buildings and tramping ancient streets with days by the pool or on the beach.

An afternoon siesta will help young children stay up late with the Turkish children (who are often still playing in town squares until midnight). Early afternoon is also a good time to hide from the sun.

THE MEDITERRANEAN

The Mediterranean has pretty varied activities for children. It has more child-friendly beaches than any other region in Turkey, with excellent strands at Lara Beach close to Antalya, beaches around Side and the gorgeous bays at Alanya. Here, they can have the full range of watersports to enjoy, including fast-paced banana rides or the opportunity for quieter sea kayaking in the coastal shallows.

Fresh water provides the most exhilarating experience at **Köprülü Canyon** (see page 64), where older children can ride the rapids in relative safety. Antalya's refurbished waterfront area – **Antalya Beach Park** (see page 26) – has a collection of child-friendly activities. There is a water

🔺 *There are children's activities at Lara Beach*

park and a recreation area, plus lots of shady forest to play in. Other water parks can be found between Alanya (see page 19) and Side (see page 38).

Jeep safaris (see page 54) are great fun for older children. Routes take you off road and offer a real 'Indiana Jones' experience.

BEWARE

The Turkish sun is very hot and can damage young skin easily. Always ensure children wear a high-factor sun cream. Reapply this regularly, especially after they have been in the water.

Limit the time children spend in the sun, especially from noon through the early afternoon when it is at its strongest. Make sure they wear a hat and always carry a lightweight but long-sleeved garment for them in case shoulders and arms need covering up.

Keep children well hydrated – they may not complain of feeling thirsty but will need lots of liquid to keep them well.

Sports & activities

BOAT TRIPS

A huge flotilla of boats offers day trips and these are good value for money, with lunch and drinks included. The most popular are the trip to Olymbos (see page 76) and the trip to Manavgat Falls (see page 38). It pays to do a little research and price comparison. Tickets usually need to be booked the day before.

CLIMBING

There are excellent climbing opportunities to be found in the Taurus Mountains and the western Lycian peaks to the north and west of Antalya. However, there are no climbing schools to offer lessons, so climbing is not recommended for beginners. For more details, contact the **British Mountaineering Club**. ⓐ 177–179 Burton Road, Manchester M20 2BB ⓣ 0161 445 6111 ⓦ www.thebmc.co.uk

GOLF

The courses at Belek (see page 49) offer the most varied quality golf in the eastern Mediterranean. There is professional instruction for all ages and standards, plus a practice driving range and 9-hole courses where you can improve your stroke play.

SCUBA DIVING

The warm, clear waters around the Turkish coast make for great diving, but because of the wealth of ancient remains lying in the coastal shallows, many locations remain off limits and divers must be accompanied by registered Turkish guides or dive masters. If you are already qualified, bring your certification with you to enable you to book a guide.

If you want to learn to dive, most large resorts have schools accredited by the Professional Association of Diving Instructors (PADI), where you can be assured of good-quality training.

WALKING & HIKING

The rugged and unspoilt landscapes of Mediterranean Turkey can really be appreciated on foot. There are several really good footpaths to follow – the best are to Selge from the Köprülü Canyon (see page 65), at Olymbos to the Chimaera flames (see page 77) and along the ridge of the Olymbos Mountain range west of Antalya. Remember to take lots of water and snacks with you. Wear a hat and sensible footwear.

WATERSPORTS

You will not be short of organised watersports unless you choose a particularly quiet resort. From jet-skiing to banana boat rides, there is something for all the family at the main resort beaches.

WINDSURFING

Expert windsurfers flock to the Aegean coast of Turkey for the best conditions, but most resorts on the Mediterranean coast have small schools offering lessons and board rentals. The gentler winds certainly suit the beginner and the improver. Kite surfing is a sport that is growing in popularity.

● *Take a boat trip out to Manavgat Falls*

Festivals & events

Turkey's festivals and events reflect its fascinating and unique society. A secular republic, it is very proud of its fight for independence, marking the major events with great solemnity. However, over 90 per cent of its population are Muslim, so they also celebrate the main Islamic festivals, especially in the countryside. On top of this, Turkey holds a whole host of sporting competitions and folk festivals.

CIVIL CELEBRATIONS

23 April National Sovereignty and Children's Day celebrate the establishment of the first Grand National Assembly in 1920, which saw the end of the Ottoman Empire.

19 May Atatürk Day and Youth and Sports Day mark the beginning of the Turkish War of Independence in 1919, when Atatürk rallied the country to fight the forces who had divided Turkish territory after World War I.

30 August Victory Day celebrates the success of Turkish forces over the Greek army in 1922.

29 October Republic Day marks the date when the present Turkish republic was declared in 1923.

10 November Atatürk's Death: although not a holiday, Turks mark the day of Atatürk's death in a very poignant way. At 09.05 on 10 November, the exact time of his death, the whole country comes to a standstill for a minute of silent remembrance.

MAJOR MUSLIM CELEBRATIONS

The Muslim calendar runs on a lunar cycle different to our solar Gregorian calendar. These celebrations change date each year.

Ramazan (Ramadan)

For the entire ninth month (30 days) of the Muslim year, Muslims fast between dawn and dusk. This marks the time when Mohammed wandered in the desert and Allah revealed the verses of the Koran to him. Muslims devote Ramazan to prayer, reflection and charity.

Şeker Bayramı (She-ker Bay-ramer or the Sugar Festival)

This three-day festival celebrates the end of Ramazan. Families party together and enjoy traditional foods, particularly sugary foods such as *baklava*, pastries and *lokum*.

Kurban Bayramı

The festival that commemorates the Prophet Abraham offering his son Isaac to Allah (when Allah accepted the sacrifice of a sheep instead). It takes place during the tenth month of the Muslim year.

Other Muslim festivals

Other major and minor festivals are not necessarily holidays but are the times for special prayers and family get-togethers, including:

Aşure Günü (ah-shoo-reh gew-new) The tenth day of the Islamic lunar month of Muharrem commemorates Adam repenting his sin, the birth of the Prophet Abraham, Jonah's deliverance from the whale and the martyrdom of Islamic hero Hüseyin. Also, Turks celebrate Noah's ark coming to rest on dry land.

Mevlid-i Nebi (mehv-leed ee neh-bee) The Prophet Mohammed's birthday is celebrated with mosque illuminations and special foods.

Three other days of celebration where mosques are decorated and lit up are: **Regaib Kandili**, the 'Beginning of the Three Moons'; **Berat Kandili**, the 'Day of Forgiveness'; and **Mirac Kandili**, celebrating the Prophet Mohammed's ascent into heaven.

Circumcision ceremonies

Circumcision is an important milestone in the life of a young Turkish boy and takes place at any time between birth and the age of seven. The child is dressed in new clothes – often a bright satin suit and a light blue headdress – and then paraded around the town visiting family and friends. This was traditionally on horseback but today could be in a parade of cars that travels the streets with horns blaring. After the ceremony there is a big family party.

LIFESTYLE

OTHER FESTIVALS & EVENTS IN THE MEDITERRANEAN REGION

June

During late June and early July the **Aspendos Opera and Ballet Festival** runs a programme of international works featuring the *crème de la crème* of the performing world, performed in the Roman theatre at Aspendos (see page 62).

July

Aspendos is again the focus for the **Aspendos Folk Festival** featuring traditional Turkish music and dance.

August

Alanya hosts an **International Folk Festival** featuring mainly Turkish and eastern Mediterranean music and dance.

October

Antalya welcomes the cinematographic industry to the **Antalya Altın Portakal Film Festivali (Golden Orange Film Festival)**, probably the most important in the eastern Mediterranean basin. International arts-type films are featured.

Alanya holds an **International Triathlon** – with swimming, cycling and running on a route through the city.

● *Souvenirs for sale in Alanya*

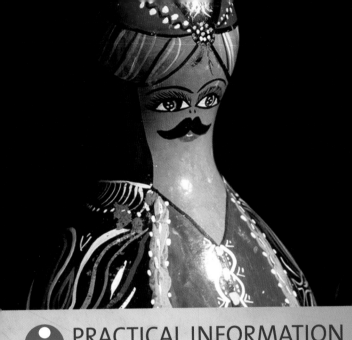

PRACTICAL INFORMATION
Tips & advice

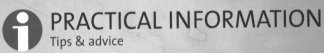

Accommodation

Hotels below are graded by approximate price for a double room for one night:

£ = under 115 YTL

££ = 115 YTL–150 YTL

£££ = over 150 YTL

ALANYA

Panorama Hotel £ The hotel lobby and restaurant is on the sea side of the main road but most of the rooms are on the other side and connected by a tunnel under the road. Half-board or full-board options available. ⓐ Keykubat Cd 30 ⓣ 0242 513 1181 ⓦ www.panoramahotel.com.tr

Bedesten Club Hotel ££ This hotel, created from an 18th-century traders' inn, has far more charm than most hotels in Alanya and is located right in the heart of the walled old town. ⓐ İç Kale ⓣ 0242 512 1234

Hillside Sü £££ Stylish design sets this hotel apart, as well as its own beach and all the facilities one would expect from a 5-star establishment. About 15 minutes from the airport. ⓐ Konyaltı ⓣ 0242 249 0700 ⓦ www.hillside.com.tr

ANTALYA

Minyon Town House ££ Charming little pension with just nine twin and double rooms, tucked away in a quiet corner of the old town. It even has its own lido, a 15-minute walk away. ⓐ Tabakhane Sk 31, Kaleiçi ⓣ 0242 247 1147

Secret Palace Pansion ££ This delightful boutique hotel is a converted Ottoman-era house, located in the most picturesque part of old Antalya. It has 11 en-suite rooms, all with air conditioning, and a garden where

orange trees surround a small pool. ⓐ Firin Sk 10, Kaleiçi ⓣ 0242 244 1060
ⓦ www.secretpalacepansion.com

BELEK

Kempinski Hotel The Dome £££ The Dome is undoubtedly the most stunning resort hotel in the Belek area, with huge pools, its own stretch of
superb sandy beach, and easy access to the Antalya Golf Course next
door. Rooms are huge and luxurious, services are superb and there is a
choice of five restaurants. ⓐ Next to Antalya Golf Club, Belek beach
ⓣ 0247 10 13 00 ⓦ www.kempinski-belek.com

SIDE

Yükser £ Orange trees in the delightful garden, traditional-style building,
good service and clean rooms. Value for money. ⓐ Sümbül Sk 4
ⓣ 0242 753 2010 ⓦ www.yukser-pansiyon.com

Sweet Home ££ There are 6 suites, 6 double rooms and 12 singles; plus
sauna, small pool and billiard room. Although 1.5 km (1 mile) from the
sea, there is a free daily transfer for guests. ⓐ 1504 Sk 2 ⓣ 0242 753 6230
ⓦ www.sweethomehotel.net

Beach House Hotel ££–£££ An attractive hotel facing the beach and
one of the nicest places to stay in Side. ⓐ Barbaros Cd
ⓦ www.beachhouse-hotel.com

Hotel Lale Park ££–£££ A homely establishment with a good restaurant
and friendly staff, very near the sea. ⓐ Lale Sk 5 ⓣ 0242 753 1131
ⓦ www.hotellalepark.com

Hotel Side Star ££–£££ Situated by the beach in the western area of Side
but close enough to the town to reach on foot. This is a good hotel, with
a range of facilities and a professional attitude towards its guests.
ⓐ Selimiye Mahallesi ⓣ 0242 753 5600 ⓦ www.sidestarhotels.com

Preparing to go

GETTING THERE

Mediterranean Turkey features in the brochures of several major package tour operators. Thomas Cook and its rival Thomson/TUI dominate the market, so there is little competition and cheap, last-minute deals are rare. British visitors are outnumbered in most of the region's resorts by Russians, Germans and other European visitors, and by well-off Turks, so prices tend to be higher than in the Aegean and Lycian regions, and are at their highest from June to September.

Most large hotels deal directly with tour operators, and booking through the internet is unlikely to turn up any outstanding bargains. Beware: if you do find a hotel in Mediterranean Turkey that offers really cheap online rates, it almost certainly has been rejected by the major tour companies because it does not come up to their standards. That said, many delightful smaller hotels, often in charming restored buildings in the historic parts of older towns, can be found online; some can also be found in the Turkey section of
Ⓦ www.specialplacestostay.com

By air

Most visitors to Turkey's Mediterranean coast arrive at Antalya International Airport, a large, modern airport located about 10 km (6 miles) east of the city centre, on the main Antalya-Alanya highway.

Transfers to Antalya and Belek take about 20–30 minutes, transfers to Side and Kemer take about an hour and transfers to Alanya about 90 minutes. Thomas Cook and Thomson/TUI both sell flight-only tickets to Antalya from most main UK regional airports, as well as package holidays. Monarch Airlines also flies from several UK regional airports. All three airlines start weekly charter flights as early as April and continue until the end of October. British Airways run frequent flights from London Gatwick to Antalya. Alternatively, you can fly to Dalaman Airport, about three hours' drive from Antalya, which is served by all three of these airlines.

British Airways Ⓦ www.britishairways.com
Monarch Airlines Ⓦ www.monarch.co.uk
Thomas Cook Ⓦ www.thomascook.com/flights/
Thomson TUI Ⓦ http://flights.thomson.co.uk

Many people are aware that air travel emits CO_2, which contributes to climate change. You may be interested in the possibility of lessening the environmental impact of your flight through the charity Climate Care, which offsets your CO_2 by funding environmental projects around the world. Visit Ⓦ www.jpmorganclimatecare.com

TOURISM AUTHORITY

For more information about Turkey before you leave, contact the **Turkish Culture and Tourism Office** (ⓔ 4th Floor, 29–30 St James's Street, London SW1A 1HB ⓣ 020 7839 7778 ⓕ 020 7925 1388 Ⓦ www.gototurkey.co.uk).

BEFORE YOU LEAVE

Holidays are supposed to be relaxing, so take a little time and plan ahead. You do not need inoculations to travel to Turkey but it would be wise to make sure that your family is up to date with shots like tetanus. It is also worth having a dental check-up before you go.

It is sensible to carry a small first-aid kit with items such as painkillers, treatment for upset stomachs, travel/sea-sickness tablets, plasters, antiseptic ointment and insect repellent. Sun cream is more expensive in Turkey, so buy this before you go. If you take any prescription medication make sure you have enough for the duration of your holiday.

ENTRY FORMALITIES
Documents

The most important documents you will need are tickets and passports. Make sure that passports for all members of the family are up to date. These can take up to 28 days to be issued by the passport office, although you can pay more for a quicker service. If your passport has less than three months to run on the date you arrive in Turkey, you need to renew it before you go. For further information on how to renew your passport and for current processing times, get in touch with the **Identity & Passport Service** (☎ 0870 521 0410 Ⓦ www.ips.gov.uk). All visitors to Turkey require a visa, which is issued on arrival and costs £10, payable in sterling or euros. Queue up for your visa before getting in line for passport control. A multi-entry tourist visa is valid for 90 days, and allows you to leave and re-enter as often as you like during that period.

Keep passports and travel tickets or confirmations in a safe place. If possible, keep photocopies of your passport numbers and ticket information (and traveller's cheques if you take them) separately.

If you are going to hire a car while in Turkey, all named drivers need to have their driving licences with them.

MONEY

You can change sterling, euros or dollars into Turkish lira at the airport exchange office on arrival. Otherwise, if you need to change currency, banks can be found in all major towns. There are plenty of exchange bureaux in resorts. Before you change money check the exchange and commission rates. In many resorts, shopkeepers and restaurateurs will happily accept payment in euros, though you will be given any change in lira and the conversion rate will not be in your favour. Sterling is not widely accepted. You will find cashpoints in the larger resorts and there are ATMs (cash machines) at all the airports.

ATMs These are widespread in the resort areas. You can obtain cash with either your Maestro Card or credit card provided you have a Personal Identification Number (PIN). Your bank or credit card company may charge more for this service.

Credit cards These are becoming more widely accepted in shops and restaurants but not in cheaper *lokantas* and *pide* stalls or in the markets, so do not rely on this as your only method of payment.

❶ You can often pay in pounds rather than in Turkish lira, so it pays to take some British cash; remember to keep this secure.

Currency The Yeni (New) Turkish Lira or YTL comes in note denominations of 1, 5, 10, 20, 50 and 100 lira. Each Yeni lira is made up of 100 kuruş, which come in coins of 1, 5, 10, 25 and 50 kuruş. There is also a 1 lira coin.

Prepaid cash cards Prepaid cash cards, such as Thomas Cook's Cash Passport (www.cashpassport.com), are a safe and cost-effective way of carrying your holiday money. You simply load the card with as much money as you like, and use it to withdraw local currency from ATM machines using your PIN. The advantage of this system is that if the card is lost or stolen, it cannot be used to gain access to any of your other accounts, and it can be frozen with a single phone call to the issuer. You can also top the card up with more credit by phone or online while you are abroad.

CLIMATE

The coastal areas of western Turkey have a Mediterranean climate. This means long, hot dry summers, mild winters with some rain, and short, warm springs and autumns.

Average daytime temperatures are: April 20°C (68°F); May 24°C (75°F); June 29°C (84°F); July 31°C (88°F); August 32°C (90°F); September 29°C (84°F); October 24°C (75°F).

In summer you will only need light clothing – breathable and natural fabrics are best – but take lightweight trousers and a long-sleeved shirt to cover your arms and legs in case you get sunburnt.

Early or late in the season take a warmer layer such as a light fleece just in case it gets a bit chilly in the evenings.

BAGGAGE ALLOWANCE

Each airline sets its own luggage allowances and these now vary widely, so it's essential to check with your airline or tour operator before you travel – get it in writing if possible. As a guideline, you can expect to be allowed at least 15 kg (33 lb) of checked luggage (bags that go in the hold) and 10 kg (22 lb) of carry-on luggage. However, most airlines now allow only one item of checked luggage per passenger free of charge, and some airlines now charge extra for all checked luggage. If you do need to pay, make sure you do so in advance, as there may be very high charges for extra luggage at check-in. Most airlines carry folding wheel-chairs free of charge, but you are likely to be charged extra for golf clubs, surfboards and other bulky items of sports kit.

During your stay

AIRPORTS

There is good road access to the region's airports, but if you are returning a rental car at the end of your holiday allow plenty of time to reach the airport and check in for your flight. If your flight departs at night, the airport will have limited facilities during your wait, so it might be wise to take drinks and snacks. Also, duty-free shops may not be open at night.

COMMUNICATIONS

Most resorts have modern public phone boxes that will offer international direct dialling to the UK. These will operate with major credit cards or phone cards that can be purchased at press kiosks, tourist offices and post offices.

Your personal mobile phone should also work, though the cost of calls is a lot higher than local rates at home. Check this with your service provider before you leave.

TELEPHONING TURKEY

To call Turkey from the UK, dial 00 90 followed by the city code (without the initial 0), then the 7-digit number.

TELEPHONING ABROAD

To call an overseas number from Turkey, dial 00 followed by the country code (UK = 44) and the area code (minus the initial 0), then the rest of the number.

USEFUL TELEPHONE NUMBERS
- **Long-distance operator** 131
- **International reverse charge calls** 115
- **International directory enquiries** 161

Most upmarket and resort hotels will offer international direct dialling that will allow you to phone home from your room, but beware of these, as they often charge a high premium. Ask about rates before making the call.

Post

Post offices have yellow signs with the black letters PTT on them. Most post offices are open government office hours and offer postal and telecommunications services. Most shops selling postcards will also sell stamps for a small price premium. A postcard to Europe or the USA costs 0.80 YTL and will take up to a week to arrive.

CUSTOMS

There are no local customs that visitors should be especially aware of because in coastal resort areas Turkish people have become very accustomed to overseas visitors. Turkey, though, is generally a conservative country and excessive behaviour of any kind is frowned upon.

DRESS CODES

Beachwear is best kept to the beach; nude bathing is not acceptable. Restaurants do not have dress codes but smart-casual attire is appropriate for an evening meal in a non-buffet restaurant.

ELECTRICITY

Power is 220 volts, 50 hertz. Plugs are European style with two round pins so you will need an adapter for your electrical appliances.

EMERGENCY NUMBERS
Fire 110
Police 155
Ambulance 112

EMBASSIES & CONSULATES
The British Embassy ⓐ Şehit Ersan Cd 46/A, Çankaya, Ankara
ⓣ 0312 455 3344

GETTING AROUND
Car hire
The easiest way to rent a car is through the internet. A good and reliable Turkish company to use is Decar (ⓦ www.decar.com) with a pick-up at the airport. An up-to-date map of Turkey's west coast is available from Roger Lascelles (ⓦ www.rogerlascellesmaps.co.uk).

You will need to leave a deposit and show your driving licence. For all car rentals, make sure you get a contact telephone number in case you have mechanical problems. Drivers must be over 21 years of age (some companies 25 years) and have held a full licence for at least one year.

Driving
In Turkey you drive on the right and overtake on the left (the opposite of the UK). Speed limits are 50 km/h (31 mph) in urban areas, 90 km/h (56 mph) on main roads and 120 km/h (74 mph) on motorways and dual carriageways – unless the signs indicate another limit. Seat belts are compulsory in front seats and back seats where fitted.

The main coast road and other major roads are generally in good condition, but small roads vary in quality and some are dirt surface rather than asphalt.

You will meet all kinds of traffic on the roads, from large, modern trucks to donkey and carts (and the occasional loose farm animal). You will need to be on the alert for slower-moving vehicles. Slower traffic will usually move onto the hard shoulder to allow you to pass.

If Turkish drivers want to cross the traffic, they will often pull over to the right and let traffic behind them pass before making the turn so they do not hold everyone up.

When traffic is quieter (at night and on Sundays), Turkish traffic lights are switched to flashing amber. This means that you will need to pay attention because there is a junction or crossroads ahead that is not controlled.

Parking is a problem in all the major resorts. Do not park where you see a yellow kerb.

You will find both leaded and unleaded petrol. Not all fuel stations are self-service. A member of staff may come and clean your windscreen. This is at no extra cost, but staff will appreciate a small tip. Some petrol stations do not accept credit cards.

Local buses

The *dolmuş* is the lifeblood of local transport. These small mini-vans run set routes, leaving the terminus when full and picking up passengers anywhere along the route. There will usually be a service from town to the main beaches and resort hotels. They are cheap and efficient.

Long-distance bus services

All Turkish towns and cities are served by an efficient, modern and cheap bus network that makes an excellent framework for touring the country. The services feature air conditioning, videos (in Turkish, of course), refreshments and programmed stops for meals.

HEALTH, SAFETY & CRIME

Turkey is a safe country and you are very unlikely to find yourself the victim of a serious incident. However, petty crime such as theft can be guarded against with a few simple rules:

- Don't carry large amounts of cash or valuables with you. Take only what you need for the day.
- Leave nothing on show in your car.
- Don't leave valuables unguarded on the beach or at cafés.
- Keep to well-lit streets at night.
- If you are unsure of the route back to your hotel or apartment, take a taxi.
- Be sure to report any stolen credit cards to the credit-card company immediately.

- Report any stolen passport to your nearest embassy or consulate immediately.

Should you require medical help, most hotels will have a doctor on call but you will be charged for the consultation (you can usually claim this back from your holiday insurance policy).

Hospital If you need to stay in hospital, there are clean, though limited, facilities in most large towns, smaller clinics in smaller towns. Staff are well trained and most doctors can speak some English. You have to pay for treatment, but depending on circumstances this could be organised directly through your insurance company. If you have travelled on a package holiday with a major tour company, your resort representative will be able to offer advice and help.

***Ezcane* (Pharmacies)** Pharmacists in Turkey are highly qualified and most will speak some English. They will be able to advise you on treatments for complaints such as minor sunburn, upset tummy, insect bites and diarrhoea. Normal opening hours are from 09.00 to 19.00 hours and there will be a duty pharmacist available in every town.

Water Although tap water is clean, only drink bottled or boiled water.

MEDIA

The English-language edition of the Turkish daily newspaper, *Zaman*, can be found in Antalya, Side and Kemer, and the *Sunday Times*, printed in Istanbul, can also be found on the day of publication. The popular English tabloids are widely available in all the leading resorts at a price premium, though they may be a day old. Most upmarket hotels will offer *BBC News 24* as part of their programming. Resort bars will often transmit Premier League matches live, and show English news reports. You will find internet cafés in most resorts.

OPENING HOURS

Opening hours for museums and archaeological sites change all the time. It is probably best not to arrive too early or too late at a site in case the ticket office is closed. For most places in Turkey, as with the rest of the Mediterranean, it is best to avoid arriving during the lunch hours, as most places will shut for a long lunch. Also be aware of seasonal variations – in the off-season, many places will shut entirely or have reduced hours.

Archaeological sites 🕐 08.00–18.00 or 19.00 (summer)

Banks 🕐 08.30–12.00 & 13.30–17.00 Mon–Fri

Government offices 🕐 08.30–12.30 & 13.30–17.30 Mon–Fri

Shops 🕐 09.00–19.00 Mon–Sat; tourist shops in resorts 09.00–22.00 (summer)

State museums 🕐 08.30–17.30 Tues–Sun; closed for lunch (winter)

RELIGION

Turkey is a predominantly Muslim country, though it is one of the most liberal Islamic populations in the world. Alcohol and gambling are allowed. The countryside is generally more conservative than the coastal resorts. If you are travelling away from the coast, or wanting to visit mosques or churches, modest dress would be appropriate and respectful.

SMOKING

Since 2008, smoking has been banned in enclosed public places such as (indoor) restaurants, airport terminals, public transport, offices and the public areas of hotels. Smoking is still permitted in the open-air sections of cafés, bars and restaurants, and in designated hotel rooms.

TIME DIFFERENCES

Turkey is two hours ahead of Greenwich Mean Time (GMT) from April until October, and one hour ahead during winter.

TIPPING

In restaurants, it is advisable to leave 10–15 per cent of the bill, plus some small change for the waiting staff. In cafés and bars, leave a tip of small change. Bell-boys should receive 50 kuruş (see Currency, page 116) per bag, room cleaners in hotels should be left 50 kuruş per day, and shoe guardians in mosques welcome a small tip.

TOILETS

There are public toilets (marked with a large, red WC symbol) wherever you would expect to find them in larger towns, such as bus stations, markets, main city squares, museums, archaeological sites and popular public beaches (where there are also usually public showers). These are usually kept fairly clean by an attendant (who will also offer you a few squares of toilet paper and a splash of cologne after you've washed your hands) but toilets are often of the basic 'squatter' type. There is a surprisingly high charge for these public WCs: in 2009, the going rate varied between 50 kuruş and 1 YTL (approximately 25–50p). Toilet facilities in bars, cafés, restaurants and hotels are usually a little more modern and sometimes cleaner.

TRAVELLERS WITH DISABILITIES

Provision for travellers with disabilities is patchy. Most new hotels and public buildings including airports have adequate wheelchair access, and some resorts have boardwalk access to their beaches. Archaeological sites and historic buildings are mostly inaccessible to wheelchair users. Facilities such as audio guides for people with visual disabilities, and induction loops for hearing-aid users, are virtually non-existent.

The company Tourism For All (ⓐ c/o Vitalise, Shap Road Industrial Estate, Kendal, Cumbria LA9 6NZ ⓣ 0845 124 9971 ⓦ www.tourismforall.org.uk) can help with general advice for travellers with disabilities, although it has no specific information on Turkey.

ACKNOWLEDGEMENTS

The publishers would like to thank the following for providing their copyright photographs for this book:
Big Stock Photos pages 23 (Eray Haciosmanoglu), 57 (Can Balcioglu), 61 (Steve Estvanik); Flickr/Timo pages 10–11; Hotel Lara Beach Resort pages 27, 105; Pictures Colour Library pages 5, 40, 111; www.sargasso-travelimages.com page 42; Thomas Cook pages 13, 20, 37, 46, 49, 53, 58, 87, 95; Turkish Tourism & Culture page 64; Wikimedia Commons pages 9 (Zeynel Cebeci), 72, 78 (Renato Valterza), 81, 87 (Mila Zinkova), 107 (Thomas Gensler); World Pictures/Photoshot pages 69, 71, 93.

Project editor: Catherine Burch
Layout: Trevor Double
Proofreader: Karolin Thomas
Indexer: Amanda Jones

Send your thoughts to
books@thomascook.com

- Found a beach bar, peaceful stretch of sand or must-see sight that we don't feature?

- Like to tip us off about any information that needs a little updating?

- Want to tell us what you love about this handy little guidebook and more importantly how we can make it even handier?

Then here's your chance to tell all! Send us ideas, discoveries and recommendations today and then look out for your valuable input in the next edition of this title.

Email to the above address or write to:
pocket guides Series Editor, Thomas Cook Publishing, PO Box 227, Coningsby Road, Peterborough PE3 8SB, UK.

Useful phrases

English	Turkish	Approx pronunciation
	BASICS	
Yes	Evet	*Evet*
No	Hayır	*Hayer*
Please	Lütfen	*Lewtfen*
Thank you	Teşekkür ederim	*Teshekkuer ederim*
Hello	Merhaba	*Merhaba*
Goodbye	Hoşça kal	*Hoshcha kal*
Excuse me	Affedersiniz	*Af-feh-dehr-see-neez*
Sorry	Pardon	*Pahr-dohn*
That's okay	Bir şey değil	*Bir shey deh-il*
I don't speak Turkish	Türkçe bilmiyorum	*Tuerkche bilmiyourum*
Do you speak English?	İngilizce biliyor musunuz?	*Inghilizh'dje biliyour musunuz?*
Good morning	Günaydın	*Guenayden*
Good afternoon	Merhaba	*Merhaba*
Good evening	İyi akşamlar	*Iyi akshamlar*
Goodnight	İyi geceler	*Iyi gedjeler*
My name is ...	Adım ...	*Adaem ...*
	NUMBERS	
One	Bir	*Beer*
Two	İki	*Eki*
Three	Üç	*Uech*
Four	Dört	*Doert*
Five	Beş	*Besh*
Six	Altı	*Alte*
Seven	Yedi	*Yedi*
Eight	Sekiz	*Sekiz*
Nine	Dokuz	*Dokuz*
Ten	On	*On*
Twenty	Yirmi	*Yirmi*
Fifty	Elli	*Elli*
One hundred	Yüz	*Yuez*
	SIGNS & NOTICES	
Airport	Havaalanı	*Hava a'lane*
Railway station	İstasyon	*Istasyon*
Platform	Peron	*Peron*
Smoking/Non-smoking	Sigara içilir/içilmez	*Sigara echilir/echilmez*
Toilets	Tuvaletler	*Tuvaletler*
Ladies/Gentlemen	Bayanlar/Erkekler	*Baianlar/Erkekler*
Underground	Metro	*Metro*